Tycoons In The Kitchen

the favorite recipes of the men who run big business

by Michael Dorn

Drawings by ROSALIND RUST

for JACKIE AND PHILIP ROLLHAUS

TABLE OF CONTENTS

INDEX OF TYCOONS

INDEX OF COMPANIES

FOREWORD

What is the tycoon doing in the kitchen? Cooking, of course — and why not? To reach the top you must have the courage to do as you please. Tycoons, by definition, have reached the top and believe, with Churchill, that courage is the quality that guarantees all the rest.

Cooking is an avocation tailor-made for tycoons. It releases the mind from the burdens of the office, frees the hands from the tedious handling of tax forms and money, satisfies the compulsion to make decisions, and fulfills the universal desire to create. The investment is safe and small and the profits come sweet and fast.

This book contains the favorite recipes of a variety of "tycoons." Some are the heads of huge empires that are known throughout the world. Others run businesses that are rarely heard of outside their own locality. Some are fabulously rich. Others are not. But none is poor and none lacks courage, and all have one thing in common — a passionate love for good food. In this book they share that love with all who like to eat.

HOW TO USE THIS BOOK

All of the recipes have been arranged to serve six moderately hungry guests during the course of a dinner — unless specifically noted to the contrary. If you decide to eliminate the first course from your dinner or lunch, you might consider increasing the quantities used in your second course.

TWENTY-ONE PRESIDENTIAL DINNERS

A Party Dinner for All Seasons

The Menu:

Quiche Beauvaisienne
Gene's Lobster Diavolo
Rice or Egg Noodles
Tossed Green Salad
Strawberry Meringue

The contributors: Mr. T. F. Willers, Hooker Chemical; Mr. Eugene J. Sullivan, Borden Chemical; Mr. Henry Ford II, Ford Motor Company; Mr. John L. Lemme, Radio KLTF.

QUICHE BEAUVAISIENNE

This dish is a glorious mixture of such basic ingredients that you will wonder why you haven't heard of it before (if you haven't), and so will your guests. As a first course for dinner or a main course at lunch, or even served cold at breakfast it is sure to delight. I list it as a first course here, for it prepares the palate in the kindest way for the lobster that is to follow it.

The recipe is from Mr. T. F. Willers, President of Hooker Chemical Corporation. It is a dish that he enjoys cooking himself as well as ordering wherever he can find it. He and his wife first encountered it on a trip to Europe more than 10 years ago. While motoring through northern France they stopped in a small restaurant known as Pignon Pointu, in the lovely town of Beauvais. The restaurant is not starred in the *Guide Michelin,* but is, Mr. Willers tells us, an excellent place for the wayfarer who likes good French food, well prepared and well served, but without a three or four hour delay.

There are many variations on quiche. Perhaps the most famous is Quiche Lorraine, which uses bacon instead of ham, does not include cheese, and sometimes calls for onions. Quiche Beauvaisienne, as a first course, will serve eight people. As a main course at lunch one pie will serve four.

Chilled chablis is Mr. Willer's suggestion for wine, and this will go perfectly with Mr. Sullivan's Lobster Diavolo, which follows the Quiche.

What You Will Need

1 pie shell, unbaked	12 ounces heavy cream
2 thick slices cooked ham (½" thick)	3 eggs
2 thick slices swiss cheese (½" thick)	1 ounce butter
	1 pinch salt

1. Heat the oven to 375F.
2. Cut the ham and the cheese into ½ inch squares and spread them on the crust.
3. Beat the three eggs thoroughly but gently with a fork.
4. Gradually blend in the cream and the salt.
5. Pour the egg and cream mixture over the ham and cheese.
6. Cut the butter into small pieces and scatter over the top.
7. Bake the Quiche for 30 to 35 minutes.
8. Remove the Quiche and let it cool until just barely warm. Slice it and serve. A Quiche for breakfast, by the way, is the Platonic idea of a ham omelette.

GENE'S LOBSTER DIAVOLO

Lobster, like beef and oysters, is the favorite of many tycoons, and this unusual recipe is the creation of Mr. Eugene J. Sullivan, President of the Borden Chemical Co. and Vice President of the Borden Co. The suggestion of frozen lobster tails is made only because they are always easy to find, and fresh lobster is often difficult to find. The frozen tails are superb with Mr. Sullivan's sauce.

What You Will Need

4 tbsps. olive oil
6 cups peeled whole tomatoes sieved
   (or 3 cups tomato sauce)
2½ tsps. salt
2 tsps. oregano
1 tsp. garlic powder

1 tsp. crushed red pepper
3 cups (28 ounce jar)
   Borden's "None Such" Mince Meat
½ cup dry red wine
6 live lobsters, 2 lbs. each
   (or 12 frozen lobster tails)

1. Heat the olive oil in a large saucepan over a medium flame.
2. Stir in the sieved tomatoes (or the tomato sauce).
3. Add the salt, pepper, garlic powder, oregano, and red pepper.
4. Bring the sauce to a boil over a high flame, stirring frequently. When the sauce reaches the boiling point, reduce the heat and simmer for 15 minutes, or until it thickens.
5. Add the mince meat and simmer another 15 minutes. Pour the sauce over the cooked lobster or lobster tails. For instructions on how to cook live lobster, see the box below. For frozen lobster tails, follow the instructions on the package.

How To Cook Live Lobster

A live lobster should have 3 to 4 quarts of water to boil in, so if you are serving 6 you will need a huge kettle or several large ones. Bring the water to a rapid boil. Plunge the lobsters in, head first, and bring to a boil again and cover. Reduce the heat and simmer for 20 minutes. Remove from the heat and drain.

With a sharp knife cut the underside of each lobster lengthwise. Cut through the thin undershell, leaving the back shell intact. Remove the dark vein from the center of the lobster and the small dark sac about two inches below the head. Crack the large claws with a nutcracker. Place the lobster, cut side up, on a warm serving platter, and cover with the hot sauce.

HENRY FORD'S FRENCH DRESSING

For a classic tossed green salad you must have a simple French dressing, and the recipe sent to me by Mr. Ford is what a French dressing ought to be. Dressings saturated with catsup and mayonnaise may please some, but not the French.

The recipe, as Mr. Ford presented it, is sufficient to serve 300, so I have reduced it to a quantity that will see you through one salad for six. French dressing does not store well and is best prepared just before serving. Remember also that it is the olive oil and the vinegar that create the inimitable flavor, and you must use the best quality that you can find. An olive oil of inferior quality will make an almost repellent dressing. First class olive oil is nearly tasteless. If you cannot find a first-class olive oil, substitute vegetable oil or peanut oil.

For the greens use a combination of Boston or romaine lettuce, watercress, chicory, and a few spinach leaves. Chopped fresh parsley is excellent. Raw onion is forbidden. Wash the greens, drain them, wrap them in a linen towel, and chill until ready to serve.

*(quantities for a salad for 6
are in parentheses)*

3 pints olive oil (¼ cup)
⅔ pint red wine vinegar (1 tbsp.)
⅓ pint cider vinegar (1 tsp.)
1 tbsp. dry French mustard (dash)
2 tbsps. sugar (¼ teaspoon)
2 dashes Lee & Perrin Sauce
   (the slightest touch)
salt, freshly ground pepper to taste,
chopped chives, chopped parsley,
and other fine herbs that are available
(See Step 4, below).
The juice of 1 clove garlic and
   1 onion (omit)

1. Dissolve the sugar and mustard in the vinegar.
2. Add the oil and the Lee & Perrin Sauce, beating with a fork.
3. Salt and pepper to taste and add the fresh parsley.
4. If you choose to use fresh herbs or spices (tarragon, basil, rosemary, etc.) add them carefully. Moderation must be observed.
5. Pour the dressing over the greens in a manner that will permit the leaves to be nicely flavored but that will leave no residue of dressing at the bottom of the bowl.
6. Toss and serve.

6

STRAWBERRY MERINGUE

Quiche Beauvaisienne and Lobster Diavolo are guaranteed to delight your guests. You must not let them down with dessert. My suggestion is the contribution of Mr. John H. Lemme of Little Falls, Minnesota. Mr. Lemme is the President of radio station KLTF and is on the boards of directors of many Minnesota companies.

Strawberry Meringue is served cold and may be prepared a day in advance.

What You Will Need

3 egg whites
½ teaspoon baking powder
1 cup sugar
Ten 2″ soda crackers crushed

½ pint of crushed pecans
1 pint of whipping cream
1 quart of whole strawberries
(fresh or frozen)

1. Heat the oven to 300F.

2. Beat the egg whites stiff and fold in the sugar and the baking powder.

3. Gently add the crushed soda crackers and the crushed pecans.

4. Grease a 9-inch baking tin and spread the mixture into it. Bake for 30 minutes.

5. Remove from oven, cool, and chill.

6. Just before serving add a quart of strawberries and top with unsweetened whipped cream.

A Simple French Dinner for Winter

The Menu:

Scallops Provençale
Carré d'Agneau Persille
Flageolet
Tossed Green Salad
Chocolate Chiffon Mold

The contributors: Mr. Clinton B. Burnett, Johns-Manville Corporation;
Mr. Albert E. Forster, Hercules Inc.; Mr. Conrad Hilton, Hilton Hotels.

What Is a Shallot?

Many French recipes call for shallots, but few stores in the United States sell them. Even in New York City they are difficult to find. It is of small importance.

A shallot might best be defined as a curious cross between an onion and garlic. It more closely resembles garlic, but it is about the size of a cherry or a grape, is covered with a thin and lavender colored skin, and has a subtle flavor that is part garlic, part onion, and part unique.

My own feeling is that shallots are unnecessary. They are a great deal of trouble to peel and slice, and if they are mixed with onions or garlic their distinctive taste is lost. To justify the trouble of obtaining them and preparing them — and their expense — they should be used alone, without onions, in dishes such as Scallops Provençale. A good compromise and a fine substitute is young green onions and a minute touch of garlic.

SCALLOPS PROVENCALE

This is a classic French dish which comes to us from Mr. Clinton Burnett, President of the Johns-Manville Corporation. Scallops Provençale are best and most striking when served in scallop shells, which can be purchased in most fish stores and cookery shops or gourmet shops for a few cents a piece. But the shell does not alter the taste, except psychologically, and if you are unable to obtain the shells use baking dishes — the individual ones. Or you may cook all of the scallops together, as you would a casserole.

If you are able to buy scallops with the little red muscle attached, sometimes known as the foot or coral, I urge that you leave it on, as the French do.

What You Will Need

1½ pounds of bay scallops
½ cup onions, chopped finely
½ cup shallots, chopped finely
 (see box for substitutes for shallots)
1 bay leaf; ¼ cup flour

1 dash of thyme
½ cup grated parmesan cheese
2 tbsps. butter
6 scallop shells
¼ cup dry white wine

1. Sauté the chopped onion and shallots in the butter until they are golden.

2. Remove them and set them aside.

3. Wash the scallops and dry them lightly with a paper or linen towel.

4. Place the flour in a clean paper bag.

5. Slip the scallops into the bag and toss them gently in the flour. Remove them from the bag and whisk away any excess flour.

6. Turn the flame on under the pan in which you sauteed the shallots and heat the remaining butter until it is foaming, adding more butter if necessary.

7. Place the scallops in the pan and brown them for two minutes.

8. Return the onions and shallots to the pan along with the wine, the bay leaf, and the thyme.

9. Place a cover on the pan and simmer gently for 3 minutes.

10. Remove the scallops from the pan, drain, and distribute the scallops and the sauce over the 6 scallop shells. Discard the bay leaf.

11. Cover each serving with a thin layer of grated parmesan cheese and a dash of butter. Note: at this point the scallops may be placed in the refrigerator until it is time for the final step — that is, five minutes before serving.

12. Just before serving, place the shells under a medium broiler for a minute or two; until they have a crisp, golden brown top. Serve immediately.

CARRE D'AGNEAU PERSILLE
(Roast Rack of Lamb With Parsley Dressing)

A rack of lamb (carré d'agneau) is a cage of ribs, and your butcher may have to reserve this cut for you, for the rib of a lamb is usually cut up, in American markets, into individual chops. The size of the rack you buy depends on the appetites of your guests. For this meal we suggest a 5- to 6-pound rack. If this is unavailable, ask for 2 racks 2½ to 3 pounds each.

This dish sends a delicate, mouth-watering aroma through the house and leaves the marvelous taste of rosemary in your mouth. It was suggested by Mr. Albert E. Forster, just retired as President and Chairman of the Board of Hercules Inc. He remembers the recipe from Gertrude Crum's "Menus By Mail," and with Mrs. Crum's kind permission we repeat it here.

The recipe calls for a 30-minute roasting process, which will produce a rare piece of lamb. I like my lamb rare, but Mr. Forster prefers his well done, and cooks it for about an hour. Your best bet, I think — this is Mr. Forster's suggestion, too — is to cook the roast according to Mrs. Crum's instructions: test it when it is done, and if it is too rare for your taste, return it to the oven for 20 minutes or so.

In preparing the dressing do not exceed the instructions for the quantity of rosemary; a little goes a long way.

What You Will Need

1 rack of lamb, 5 to 6 pounds (or 2 smaller racks)	6 ounces beef consomme
1 large yellow onion	2 tbsps. butter
1 stalk of celery	½ cup finely chopped fresh parsley
2 bay leaves	1 cup breadcrumbs
½ tsp. rosemary	4 shallots (or young green onions — see box on shallots)
6 ounces white wine	

1. Preheat the oven to 400F.

2. Place the rack in a roasting pan fat-side down. Sprinkle rack liberally with salt and pepper. Roast 20 minutes.

3. Remove rack from oven and drain off all fat. Return rack to oven with sliced onion, celery in pieces, and ¼ teaspoon of the rosemary sprinkled over. Roast 10 minutes more.

4. Remove rack to platter on which you can reheat it and serve, but leave the onion and the celery in the roasting pan.

12

5. To the contents and juices of the roasting pan add white wine, consomme, and butter. Let this boil up and cook gently.

6. Make the Persillade, thusly:

    a. Sauté 4 minced shallots in butter.

    b. Add 4 slices of crumbled bread to the shallots and butter.

    c. Season with salt, pepper, and the remaining rosemary and blend thoroughly.

    d. Taste and correct, if necessary, and add the chopped parsley.

7. Spread the persillade over the bone side of the rack. Reheat and serve with the strained sauce around the rack, or serve the sauce separately. The parsley dressing should be nicely browned, and this requires close watching, for it browns quickly.

FLAGEOLET

Flageolet are little French beans that are similar to, but much smaller and tastier than lima beans. In France they are lamb's traditional holiday bedfellow.

The amateur Franchophile frequently insists that good flageolet cannot be bought in the U.S. He is wrong. Even in France this little bean is not cooked for a few minutes, like a pea. It is a dried bean which requires hours of simmering with a bit of pork and a hint of garlic or spice. The dried bean is imported to the U.S. But you need not bother with it. The canned flageolet imported from France and available in gourmet shops and even in most large supermarkets throughout the land is a superb product and a brilliant argument for canned products.

Two cans or jars should be sufficient for six. Simply heat the flageolet and serve. A slice of crisp, broiled bacon atop each serving adds an elegant touch.

OTHER VEGETABLES

There are those who deplore the serving of vegetables that have been used primarily to add their flavor to the meat, such as the celery, in this dinner, that has cooked with the lamb. Such people suggest that the celery be discarded. They do not realize that celery cooked in such a manner is identical to braised celery — another French delicacy. So by all means serve the celery.

If you want this meal to be entirely French you will want to serve a salad as a third course. Use the recipe for tossed green salad, with Mr. Ford's dressing, in Chapter I.

14

CHOCOLATE CHIFFON MOLD

This magnificent concoction of froth and chocolate is very much like, and very much easier than another French classic, the Chocolate Mousse. The recipe is the contribution of Mr. Conrad Hilton, whose hotels grace so many of the world's cities. The powdered coffee added to the whipped cream is the pièce de resistance — a real stroke of genius. The coconut may be omitted.

What You Will Need

1 envelope unflavored gelatine	2 squares unsweetened chocolate
⅔ cup sugar	½ cup whipping cream
¼ tsp. salt	1 tsp. vanilla
3 eggs	2 tsps. powdered sugar
1½ cups milk	½ cup shredded coconut

1. Mix together 1 envelope gelatine, ⅓ cup sugar, and ¼ teaspoon salt in the top of a double boiler.

2. Beat together 3 egg yolks and 1½ cup of milk and slowly add to the gelatine mixture.

3. Add 2 squares unsweetened chocolate and cook over boiling water until the chocolate is melted. Stir frequently.

4. Remove the mixture from heat and beat with a rotary beater until smooth. Chill until partially thickened.

5. Whip ½ cup of whipping cream and add to the gelatine mixture (it may need to be whipped to make it smooth). Add 1 teaspoon of vanilla.

6. Beat 2 of the egg whites until stiff and gradually fold in ⅓ cup of sugar. Fold this into the combined cream and gelatine mixture.

7. Put into a 1 quart mold.

8. Chill for at least 1 hour.

9. Just before serving, place the mold in hot water, count 10 slowly, and unmold.

10. Spread the chiffon mold with 1 cup of stiffly whipped cream to which has been added 2 teaspoons of powdered coffee and 2 teaspoons of confectioners sugar.

11. (Optional) Toast a half cup of shredded coconut until light brown and sprinkle it over the mold.

A Dinner of Surprises

The Menu:

Caviale con Fagioli
Ham Rings
Stuffed Artichokes
Watercress Salad
Mount Everest Dessert

The contributors: Mr. Daniel Parker, The Parker Pen Company; Mr. Eugene J. Sullivan, The Borden Chemical Company.

CAVIALE CON FAGIOLI

Everyone likes to be surprised, so long as it's a pleasant surprise. The courses in this dinner are exceedingly pleasant and all of them are unique.

Caviale con fagioli is an Italian dish that is a specialty of *Paoli,* one of the oldest restaurants in Florence and long one of my favorites. The dish is extraordinarily simple to make and is surprising because it marries the commonest of ingredients — the bean — to the noblest of delicacies — caviar. The result is indisputably successful.

What You Will Need

2 pounds of dry white beans
  (Great Northern are preferred)
1 clove of garlic
6 tbsps. black caviar
  (fresh or unsalted, if possible)
½ cup lemon juice

1 cup high quality olive oil
  (or peanut or vegetable oil)
3 lemons, seeded and quartered
2 thick slices of bacon
5 quarts fresh water

1. Soak the beans in fresh water for 12 hours. Distilled or bottled mineral or spring water is excellent.

2. Drain off the water — but preserve it.

3. Bring it to a boil in a large kettle and add the garlic, peeled and chopped, and the beans.

4. Boil for one hour or until done (the beans are done when they are soft and tender but retain their shape).

5. Drain the beans, cool them, and chill them. You may store them in the refrigerator for several days.

6. To serve:

   a. Distribute the beans into large, shallow soup bowls.

   b. Add 1 tbsp. oil, 1 tsp. lemon juice, and 1 tbsp. caviar to each serving.

7. Serve with lemon wedges and additional oil and lemon juice, should it be desired.

NOTE: If you like — and for even greater surprise — you may serve the beans simply in their bowls, with nothing added, and provide your guests with cruets of oil and lemon juice and a goblet of caviar. They may then mix in the caviar and dressing themselves.

HAM RINGS

Daniel Parker is Chairman of the Board of the Parker Pen Company and his recipe for Ham Rings keeps up the tone of simple, but tremendously exciting food. You will have only one problem: neither ground ham nor ground *fresh* pork is easy to find pre-packaged. But it's quite simple for your butcher to grind the meat for you, and do not hesitate to ask him. He ought to be delighted to. Do specify lean ham and pork, though. The leaner the meat the better the ultimate meal.

What You Will Need

1 pound ground ham ⎱ grind together	½ cup milk
1 pound ground pork ⎰	1½ cups brown sugar
6 pineapple rings	½ cup pineapple juice
1-1½ cups soft bread crumbs	1 tsp. dry mustard
2 eggs	

1. Heat the oven to 325F.
2. Mix the ground meat with the bread crumbs, 2 slightly beaten eggs, and the milk.
3. Form this mixture into 6 rings about the size of a pineapple ring.
4. Place the rings on a rack and cover each with a pineapple ring, and bake for 1¼ hours.
5. Start to baste the rings with a sauce made of:
   - a. 1½ cups brown sugar
   - b. 1 tsp. dry mustard
   - c. ½ cup tarragon vinegar
   - d. ½ cup pineapple juice
6. Continue the basting process for 20 minutes. Remove the rings from the oven and serve.

STUFFED ARTICHOKES

Here is a delightful and easy way to have artichokes. It is easy for the cook *and* for the guests, who will not be bothered with the labors involved in eating a boiled artichoke.

What You Will Need

6 small artichokes	1 cup cooked green peas
2 cups chicken broth	1 tsp. salt
6 chicken livers	2 tbsps. olive oil
¼ cup chopped onion	1 clove garlic

1. Place the garlic, olive oil, and salt in a large kettle containing 4 quarts of water. Bring the water to a boil.

2. While the water is heating, rinse the artichokes with cold water, cut off the stems, and trim the leaves slightly with a scissors. Tear off the lower, loose-hanging leaves and slice each of the artichokes in half, lengthwise.

3. Slip the artichokes into the boiling water, reduce the heat, and simmer for 25 minutes.

4. As the artichokes simmer, chop up the chicken livers and saute them in butter for five minutes.

5. Remove the livers and mince them together with the onions.

6. Gently blend the cooked peas into the liver and onion paste. Set the mixture aside.

7. Drain the artichokes, and when they have cooked enough for you to handle them remove the choke — the fibrous pulp in the center — with a spoon.

8. Stuff the liver paste into the center of each artichoke.

9. Arrange the stuffed artichokes in a flat baking dish, add the chicken broth, and simmer covered for 15 minutes. Serve hot or cold.

WATERCRESS SALAD

The English poet William Cowper long also described watercress as "a cheap but wholesome salad from the brook," and even today the English may be seen gathering watercress from their still-unpolluted streams. For most of us the source of this plant is less enchanting, but it remains wholesome and provides a good diversion from lettuce.

The world's best watercress supply comes from the English village of Ewelme, the master of which, curiously enough, is by tradition the Regis Professor of Medicine at Oxford. Ewelme's watercress has tiny round leaves. The Italian variety has larger, and some think, less tasty leaves. Whichever variety you choose the preparation is the same: wash, drain, and chill. Do not cut off the stems. They are a necessary part of the plant.

The dressing for watercress should be as simple as possible — just oil and vinegar, or a non-glorified French dressing such as Mr. Ford's (see Chapter I).

MOUNT EVEREST DESSERT

Here is another contribution from Eugene Sullivan of Borden Chemical (his Lobster Diavolo appears in Chapter I). It is absurdly easy to do, yet gives the impression, in its final state, of having required supreme talent and energy.

It is a rich dessert, however. You might prefer to leave out the coconut or the whipped cream topping. It is good frozen, with a few fresh berries sprinkled on top each serving. Or you might reverse the order, and float a cloud of this exquisite stuff on top of a dish of berries.

What You Will Need

1⅓ cups (15 ounce can) Borden's
    Eagle Brand Sweetened
    Condensed Milk
⅓ cup fresh lemon juice

1 tbsp. grated lemon rind
2 cups sour cream
2 cups flaked coconut (optional)
½ pint heavy cream (excessive)

1. In a large bowl, blend the sweetened condensed milk, the lemon juice, and the grated rind.
2. Fold in the sour cream and the coconut, if you are using it.
3. Spoon into individual parfait glasses or dessert dishes.
4. Chill in the refrigerator for 2 hours — or freeze it.
5. If you like, serve topped with whipped sweetened cream.

An International Dinner

The Menu:

Madrilène à la Russe
Szekeley Goulas
Apple Sauce
Tomatoes Vinaigrette
Sherry Trifle

The contributors: Mr. Clinton B. Burnett, Johns-Manville Corporation; Miss Julie Mayes, The Turks Head Inn.

MADRILENE A LA RUSSE

This meal begins with a Russian soup, moves onto a Hungarian goulash, proceeds with a German salad, and finishes off with a famous English pudding.

Madrilène à la Russe is a clever and economical way to serve caviar to people who think they do not like caviar. And although salmon roe, or red caviar, is not nearly the delicacy that fresh, black sturgeon caviar is, the red variety is a fraction of the price, very pretty, and an exotic complement to this soup.

What You Will Need

3 cans tomato madrilène	**¼ cup dry sherry**
1 medium-size jar red caviar	**1 cup whipped sour cream**

1. Chill the madrilène in its cans for as long as it takes to jell (about six hours). Do not try to hurry the process by putting the madrilène into the freezer, since the water will crystalize.

2. When you are ready to call your guests to table, open the cans and pour the contents into a chilled mixing bowl.

3. Add the sherry and whip gently with a fork or egg whip.

4. Pour the soup into 6 consomme cups or sherbet glasses.

5. Place a generous teaspoon of sour cream atop each serving.

6. Cap each clump of cream with a teaspoon of red caviar.

SZEKELY GOULAS

At least a thousand recipes for "stew" the world over begin with instructions to saute the chopped onion in oil or butter until golden, then add meat. Here is another one, and we offer it without hesitation, for it has three peculiarities that make it different and exceptional, and that are bound to win praise: the nest of sauerkraut; the sprinkling of caraway seeds; and an enormously successful marriage of beef and pork.

What You Will Need

1 pound round steak	1 dash of vinegar
1 fresh pork shoulder	1 pint sour cream
3 medium size onions	1 tbsp. caraway seeds
2 tbsps. butter	salt
2 tbsps. Hungarian Rose paprika	pepper
2 pounds sauerkraut	½ cup beef broth

1. Chop the onions coarsely and sauté them until they are golden (not brown or black).

2. Add the paprika and a dash of vinegar, simmer for 10 minutes, and remove from the skillet.

3. Cut the beef and the pork into 1½ inch squares and brown them separately.

4. Set the pork aside and simmer the beef, onions, and paprika in the beef broth for 30 minutes.

5. Add the pork and caraway seeds and simmer for another 20 minutes.

6. Add the sauerkraut and simmer for an hour.

7. Spoon in the sour cream, simmer for another 5 minutes, and serve. The recipe comes from Clinton Burnett, President of the Johns-Manville Corporation.

TOMATOES VINAIGRETTE

A lettuce salad does not go well with sauerkraut, so for this dinner I suggest the salad that is so often served in the restaurants and beer cellars of Germany. The only thing to do: peel and slice six large, ripe tomatoes, arrange them on a platter, sprinkle them with French dressing (Chapter I) and a few capers, decorate the platter with a few sprigs of parsley, chill, and serve.

SHERRY TRIFLE

There is no excuse for a bad trifle. But English tea rooms and American cafeterias are notorious for putting out atrocious concoctions. Do not emulate them. Put a little love into this simple dish and you will win rounds of applause and many encores.

The recipe is from Julie Mayes, a devastating Britisher who runs the Turks Head Inn on Grand Turk Island, in the West Indies.

Miss Mayes is the first lady tycoon in this book, and her recipe is one that hardly lets down her sex.

What You Will Need

1 small cake (white, sponge, or angelfood)	1 tsp. sugar
	1 tsp. vanilla extract
3 cups of fresh fruit (berries, melon, citrus fruits, etc.)	1 cup heavy cream
	¼ cup walnuts
1 cup sweet sherry	6 maraschino cherries
½ pint of milk	1 cup grape or strawberry jam
2 eggs	

1. Divide the cake in half, spread with the jam, and put the cake together again. Cut it into 1 inch cubes.

2. Line the bottom of 6 goblets with the cake and dampen the cake with a sprinkling of sherry.

3. Add a layer of fresh fruit to the goblet.

4. Repeat the layers of cake, sherry, and fruit, and finish with a layer of cake (one goblet usually holds two layers of fruit, three of cake — this depends on the size of the goblet).

5. Make a custard, this way:

    a. Heat 1 cup of milk until luke warm.

    b. Beat 2 eggs thoroughly with a fork and add the milk to them. Return to sauce pan. (If you rinse the pan with cold water before returning the egg and milk mixture you will avoid sticking).

    c. Heat the mixture, stirring constantly until it coats the back of a spoon. Do not boil it. Cooking the custard too quickly will cause it to curdle and the result will resemble scrambled eggs. If this happens the lumps may be beaten out with a whisk.

    d. Add 1 teaspoon of sugar and a drop of vanilla extract. Cool the custard.

6. Pour the cooled custard over the top layer of the cake and allow it to seep through onto the fruit and down to the bottom of the goblet. This will give a handsome marbled appearance to the glass.

7. Place the dessert in the refrigerator and let it set for about two hours.

8. Whip the cream and scoop it on top of the custard and decorate with the nuts and cherries.

A Dinner for Any Occasion

The Menu:

Orange Borscht
Tarragon Chicken
Egg Noodles
Tomato and Mushroom Salad
Berries Everett Street

The contributors: Mr. John Walker, The National Gallery of Art; Mr. Vidal Sassoon, Vidal Sassoon Ltd.

ORANGE BORSCHT

This is an attractive and tasty soup and is best cold. It makes an excellent first course for any meal. The recipe is from Mr. John Walker, Director of the National Gallery of Art in Washington, D.C.

What You Will Need

3 cups of grated beets	1 cup fresh orange juice
4½ cups beef bouillon	1 cup sour cream
1½ cups tomato juice	2 tbsps. chopped chives
½ teaspoon thyme	salt and pepper to taste

1. Grate enough unpeeled beets to make 3 cups (about 5 large beets).
2. Place the beets and the beef bouillon into a stainless steel or enamel sauce pan and simmer for 20 minutes.
3. Strain out the beets and add to the bouillon 1½ cups of tomato juice, 1 teaspoon of salt, and ½ teaspoon each of thyme and pepper.
4. Bring the mixture to a boil and add 1 cup of strained, fresh orange juice.
5. Serve the borscht hot or cold, garnished with a puff of sour cream and a few chopped chives.

TOMATO AND MUSHROOM SALAD

The use of "raw" mushrooms in a salad is, so far as I know, an Italian invention, and a salad made only of a variety of the dazzlingly huge mushrooms of Italy is very pleasing.

To remind yourself of Rome:
1. Take 6 large tomatoes, peel, slice, and arrange on a serving platter. Top with a few drops of oil and vinegar.
2. Slice 12 large white mushrooms and arrange them on top of the tomatoes.
3. Add a little more oil and a touch of vinegar, and sprinkle on salt, pepper, and a few capers. Chill and serve.

CHICKEN TARRAGON

Vidal Sassoon is well known as a hair stylist and manufacturer of beauty products. His recipe presents only one problem: the search for fresh tarragon. If you do not grow your own in a window box, try to locate a source. It is well worth the trouble, for a substitution removes the special flavor. Dried tarragon can be used in a pinch.

What You Will Need

1 large boiling chicken	1 tbsp. butter
2 carrots	1 tbsp. flour
2 onions	1 egg
3 tbsps. butter	a few sprays of fresh tarragon
1½ pints water or chicken stock	salt and pepper
1 clove	

1. Slice the carrots and onions and place them in a deep roasting pan. Stuff the butter and chopped tarragon leaves inside the bird, sew the bird up, and place it on top of the carrots and onions.

2. Pour in the water or stock until it comes half-way up the side of the chicken.

3. Add the salt, pepper, clove, and a small sprig of tarragon. Cover and roast slowly until tender (3 hours in a 300F oven).

4. When the bird is cooked, skin it and set it aside.

5. Strain the stock and cook it rapidly to reduce it, gradually adding more butter and flour until you have a creamy sauce.

6. Beat the egg and blend it into the sauce together with a few additional tarragon leaves.

7. Pour the sauce over the chicken and serve it with hot egg noodles. Decorate with a tarragon sprig.

BERRIES EVERETT STREET

Vidal Sassoon is particularly fond of yoghurt and fresh fruit, and stresses that he never uses white sugar, only brown. I think he would find this dessert made for him. It was invented by an academic tycoon who lives on Everett Street, in Cambridge, Massachusetts, and abhors publicity.

What You Will Need

1 pint fresh blueberries	1 pint plain yoghurt
1 pint fresh strawberries	2 tablespoons brown sugar

A Dinner for Autumn

The Menu:

Angels on Horseback
"More"
Tycoon Salad
Lemon Sherbet with Creme de Menthe

The contributors: Mr. R. T. Parfet Jr., The Upjohn Company; Mr. Fred Foy, Koppers Company.

ANGELS ON HORSEBACK

In England, Angels on Horseback is traditionally served as a savoury — a dish served after the main course and the salad, sometimes following the dessert, sometimes replacing it. Angels on Horseback makes just as good a first course as it does a savoury — and is a real winner as a canape.

This recipe is the favorite of Mr. R. T. Parfet Jr., the President of Upjohn Company of Kalamazoo, Michigan.

What You Will Need

3 dozen large oysters, shelled	1 tsp. paprika
18 slices of thin bacon	salt and pepper to taste
2 tbsps. finely chopped parsley	6 lemon wedges

1. Drain the oysters. Be careful to remove all shell particles.

2. Cut the bacon slices in half and spread them out on a mixing board.

3. Place one oyster in the center of each bacon slice and sprinkle with the seasonings and the parsley.

4. Wrap the bacon around the oyster and secure with a toothpick.

5. Place the oysters and their bacon coverings on a rack in a shallow baking pan and bake six to eight minutes, or until the bacon is crisp, in a 450F oven.

6. Serve the Angels hot with the lemon wedges.

"MORE"

Entire books have been written on the *casserole,* and more will follow, because a casserole is a meal in one dish, requires little effort, is universally liked, and is always useful — whether on a picnic, stored in the freezer, for a pot luck dinner, or even at a fancy banquet.

This casserole — "More" — is the contribution of Mr. Fred Foy, Chairman of the Board of the Koppers Company of Pittsburgh.

Mr. Foy recommends that his casserole be served with hot French bread and a bottle of red wine. The recipe, an old California one, is superb just as it is, but if you sprinkle a few crushed corn flakes or soda crackers on top, along with the grated cheese, you will get a nice crust to give the illusion that the inside is soft and tender (the inside *is* soft and tender). If you want to be especially fancy, add pineapple chunks, mushrooms, and a drop of sherry.

What You Will Need

1 pound of noodles (any variety)	1 can of pimientos
2 large onions, minced	1 can of tomato sauce
¼ cup cooking oil	1 can of pitted ripe olives
2 pounds ground round steak	1 pound sharp cheddar cheese
1 large can of whole tomatoes	salt and pepper to taste
1 can of peas	Optional: Chrushed pineapple,
1 pinch of oregano	button mushrooms, dash of sherry
1 can of whole kernal corn	

1. Boil the noodles according to the instructions on the package, drain them, and set them aside.

2. Preheat the oven to 325F.

3. Sauté the onions slowly in oil until they are golden. Remove the onions, but leave the oil in the pan.

4. Heat the oil to a high temperature and brown the meat in it, adding salt, pepper, and a pinch of oregano.

5. Return the onions to the meat and add the remaining ingredients except for the cheese. (Drain the peas, corn, olives and pimientos.)

6. Grate the pound of cheese and mix three quarters of it into the casserole. Heat this mixture until the cheese is melted. Add the noodles.

7. Spoon all of the mixture into an ovenware casserole dish, top with the remaining grated cheese, and cook for two hours in a 325F oven.

TYCOON SALAD

This is a smashing dish that has been around for so long that its origin, like that of certain outrageous words, has grown obscure. Occasionally it is called "Bean Salad," occasionally "2-Day Salad." I call it "Tycoon Salad" because the tycoons I have tested it on have given it unqualified praise. Those who call it "2-Day Salad" will tell you to let it sit in the refrigerator for 2 days before serving. Balderdash. An hour is sufficient.

What You Will Need

1 medium-size onion, finely chopped	1 large can French-cut green beans
1 green pepper, diced	½ cup olive oil
1 large can of kidney beans	½ cup red wine vinegar
1 large can yellow beans	½ cup sugar
1 large can green waxed beans	salt, pepper, and basil to taste

1. Dissolve the sugar in the vinegar.
2. Open the cans of vegetables and pour off the liquid.
3. Toss the vegetables, the onion, the green pepper, and the sugar, vinegar, and oil together in a large mixing bowl.
4. Season to taste with the spices.
5. Chill for one hour (or as long as you like).
6. Drain off any excess juices and serve.

One favorite of many tycoons that goes splendidly with any lunch or dinner is a good, stiff drink. Mr. Charles Willis Jr., President of Alaska Airlines, lists as his particular favorite Scotch and Water. He did not specify quantities in his instructions to us. He simply specified technique. *"Pour slowly."*

LEMON SHERBET WITH CREME DE MENTHE

3 pints lemon sherbet
  (lemon ice may be substituted)
6 generous tablespoons of creme de menthe

Scoop the sherbet into 6 parfait glasses and dribble a generous table-spoon of creme de menthe over each serving. What could be simpler? And this dessert is not at all dull. The flavor and color of the dark green mint elevates the sherbet to the category of food for the gods, and makes an appropriately light finish to a casserole dinner.

A Dinner to Make in the Morning

The Menu:

Tomatoes Capriccio
Lean Boiled Beef Browned
Boiled Potatoes
Spinach Salad
Grapes Helene

The contributors: Mr. David Sarnoff, Radio Corporation of America;
Mr. Gerald M. Jennings, Everest & Jennings Inc.

TOMATOES CAPRICCIO

I was introduced to this dish at *Capriccio's,* just off the Via Veneto in Rome. This charming restaurant is noteworthy because it has a lovely tree growing through the center of it, and because those who lunch there are shown the latest Italian fashions by beautiful Italian models who stroll, unannounced, through the restaurant, parading the latest creations.

The tomato dish described here is served as part of an elaborate cold antipasto, for which Capriccio's is famous.

Tomatoes Capriccio are a pleasant change of pace from the cold soups and seafood cocktails that usually herald a summer dinner; and their spicy flavor provides warm comfort even for a winter dinner. But they are best in the fall, when the tomatoes are big and juicy. Another advantage: they may be prepared several days in advance. Marination improves them.

What You Will Need

6 large, fresh tomatoes	1 clove garlic
2 cups cooked rice	1 tsp. tabasco sauce
2 small cans minced clams	1 tsp. oregano
1 tsp. olive oil	6 anchovies
2 tsps. tarragon vinegar	1 cup chopped mushrooms

1. Blanch the tomatoes in boiling water for 10 seconds and remove the skins.

2. Carefully hollow the tomatoes. Discard the stems and seeds but preserve the flesh. Do not remove too much of the flesh. The tomatoes must retain enough shape to be stuffed.

3. Set the tomatoes aside. While they are cooling mix all of the ingredients *except the anchovies* (but including the tomato meat) together and heat them thoroughly.

4. Coat the bottom of an ovenware casserole with ¼ cup water and ¼ cup olive oil.

5. Place the tomatoes in the casserole and stuff them with the rice, clam, and spice mixture.

6. Decorate the top of each tomato with strips of anchovies.

7. Bake for 10 minutes at 400F. Cool, chill, and serve.

LEAN BOILED BEEF BROWNED

David Sarnoff is Chairman of the Board of the Radio Corporation of America and, in turn, chief executive of its subsidiary, NBC. His favorite dish is Lean Boiled Beef Browned. It is my favorite, too — not only because it is nearly impossible to ruin, but because it lends itself to a variety of experiments. It is disgraceful simply to boil the beef in water. *Doing things* to the water makes all the difference.

Boiled beef is called by many different names but, unlike a rose, is rarely the same. The recipe below is one you can tamper with as you like. A little roast will survive almost anything you do to it. There are recipes for boiling beef in beer, whiskey, rum, and even coffee. I even know one chap who managed to ruin a boiled beef. He awoke one morning at four with the idea that he could prepare the beef before he went to his office, at nine. But he forgot the kitchen while shaving, and when he returned home that night at six the beef had been simmering for 14 hours, and there was nothing left but a charred pot and a sensational smell. (Boiled beef sends out fantastic aromas while it is simmering).

What You Will Need

5 to 6 pounds of beef (rump roast is best)	1 bottle red wine
Assortment of vegetables (carrots, onions, radishes, celery, turnips, and/or whatever is in season or tempting)	2 cups beef broth
	2 tbsps. flour
	2 tbsps. cooking oil
	1 tsp. tabasco sauce
4 cloves garlic	Spices: salt, pepper, thyme, rosemary, etc., to taste

1. Chop up the vegetables.

2. Place the vegetables and the wine and beef broth into a large kettle and bring to a boil.

3. While the liquid is coming to the boil, heat the oil in a heavy iron skillet until it is smoking.

4. Dip the roast in flour and brown it in the skillet. This process should take only a few minutes. Be careful to avoid being splattered by the hot oil.

5. Slip the beef into the boiling broth, reduce the heat, and simmer slowly for 4 to 6 hours. The beef may be simmered covered or uncovered, depending on how thick you want the broth to be.

6. Remove the roast to a platter, surround with the vegetables, and carefully cover with the broth.

SPINACH SALAD

Fresh, crisp spinach leaves are frequently found in a tossed salad, but it is rarely that one finds a salad made entirely of spinach. Mr. Gerald M. Jennings, President of Everest & Jennings, Inc. of Los Angeles, sent us this recipe. It is truly an amazing one — and don't be upset by the dressing for it, which replaces olive oil with bacon drippings.

What You Will Need

1½ bunches young spinach
(Use your judgment. Get enough to make a salad for 6 — and remember that spinach served "raw" goes tremendously farther than cooked spinach.)
6 strips of bacon

1 bunch young green onions
Dash of seasoned salt (Lawry's)
Dash of pepper
⅓ cup vinegar
Bacon drippings
4 hard boiled eggs
½ teaspoon sugar

1. Wash the spinach, drain, and wash it again to be sure that you have got rid of all sand and grit, which is difficult to chew and annoying to digest.

2. Tear the leaves into smaller pieces, drain them, wrap them in a linen towel, and store them in the refrigerator until they are crisp (or you are ready to serve them).

3. Slice the green onions, using both the bulbs and the small green tops. Set aside.

4. Cut the bacon into ½ inch strips and fry it. Be careful to avoid browning either the bacon or the fat too much.

5. Remove the bacon and drain it on a paper towel. Preserve the bacon drippings in their pan.

6. Lightly toss together the bacon, spinach, onions, and the seasonings.

7. Peel and slice the hard boiled eggs and set aside.

8. When you are ready to serve the salad, heat the bacon drippings, the vinegar, and the sugar, and pour this mixture over the salad in driblets, tossing as you pour. Garnish with the egg slices and serve.

GRAPES HELENE

Boiled beef and Tomatoes Capriccio will keep your morning busy — so, if you like, you can make this dessert the previous night — or in the afternoon, while the tomatoes are cooling and the beef boiling. It really should sit 5 hours before serving. If it sits 24 hours before serving it loses nothing. Anyway you look at it it's heaven.

What You Will Need

2 pounds of seedless white grapes
1 pint whipped sour cream
1 cup dark brown sugar

1. Spread the sour cream over the bottom of a deep, 9-inch ovenware casserole.

2. Spoon ¾ cup of dark brown sugar on top of the cream.

3. Press the grapes into the sugar and cream — but do not stir. Just keep pressing the grapes down until the pan is filled or until you run out of grapes.

4. Cover the bowl and chill.

5. Just before serving sprinkle the remaining brown sugar (¼ cup) over the top and place the casserole under the broiler for 30 or 40 seconds — just long enough to carmelize the sugar.

A Dinner for Spring

The Menu:

Melone e Prosciutto
Braised Beef
Lime Aspic
Cheese Cake

The contributors: Dr. Aurelio Peccei, Olivetti & Co. SpA; Mr. William Breakstone, Jr., Tapetron, Inc.

MELONE E PROSCIUTTO

Dr. Peccei, who for many years was Managing Director of Olivetti, the great Italian firm, did not give a recipe that was distinctively Italian. He chose braised beef. In his honor this menu starts with a particularly refreshing Italian first course.

What You Will Need

3 small ripe melons
6 lemon wedges
parsley sprigs

1. Slice the melons into quarters, remove the rind, and arrange two slices of melon on each plate.

2. Drape the prosciutto over the melon slices and serve garnished with a lemon wedge and sprigs of parsley.

NOTE: Prosciutto is a special kind of Italian ham that may be bought fresh in any Italian market, or in tins in most gourmet shops. If neither is available you may substitute any thinly sliced and highly spiced ham.

BRAISED BEEF

Dr. Peccei's recipe departs from the traditional methods of braising beef by using stew-size pieces of round steak. This makes braising considerably easier and the naturally tasty round steak holds its shape. For a dinner wine Dr. Peccei recommends "a good French red."

What You Will Need

8 small onions
4 carrots
1 stalk of celery
2 tbsps. olive oil
2 lbs. round steak cut in 2-inch cubes
1 cup of red wine

1 cup of cognac
salt and pepper
1 bay leaf
½ tsp. thyme
1 to 2 cups beef broth

1. Cut the carrots, celery, and onions into bite-size pieces and put them into an earthenware pot with the oil.

2. Sauté lightly, until the onions are golden in color.

3. Remove the vegetables from the pot and brown the beef.

4. Add salt, pepper, the bay leaf and the thyme, the red wine, and the cognac. Keep the fire at a medium flame. After 10 or 15 minutes, when the alcohol has boiled off and the wine has given its flavor to the meat, add a cup of beef broth and the vegetables, cover the meat, and simmer it for an hour and a half. Stir the mixture from time to time. If it appears to be drying out add more broth.

Braised beef may be served with rice, potatoes, noodles, or on toast.

LIME ASPIC

This beguiling combination of lime and cheese was invented one day by Mr. William Breakstone, Jr., President of Tapetron, Inc. The aspic may be prepared a day in advance and stored in the refrigerator. Lime Aspic is a great favorite of the Wall Street crowd, who invariably describe it as "heaven."

What You Will Need

2 packages lime gelatin
4 cups boiling water
¼ cup minced onions

¼ cup minced green peppers
1 ripe avocado
1 pound cream cheese

1. Let the cream cheese warm to room temperature.
2. Mince the onions and green peppers.
3. Bring the water to a boil.
4. Pour the gelatin into a large mixing bowl and dissolve it with the boiling water.
5. Blend the cream cheese into the mixture, leaving a few lumps if desired.
6. Blend in the onions and the green peppers.
7. Let the mixture cool. When it is cool enough to place in the refrigerator, peel and slice the avocado, arrange the slices on the bottom of a dessert mold, and pour the aspic over it.
8. Refrigerate until set — at least two hours.
9. Unmold and serve. (To unmold, place the mold in a sink of hot water for one second and turn the mold upside down on a serving platter).

BREAKSTONE'S CHEESE CAKE

Mr. William Breakstone Sr. is president of Typecraft Service, Inc. of New York City. Several firms in the printing industry in New York are headed up by members of the Breakstone family, and now Bill Breakstone Sr.'s son, Bill Jr., has launched off on his own and started a new company, experimenting with computerized type setting, in Long Island. Tycoonsmanship *can be* hereditary.

Bill Sr.'s favorite dessert is cheese cake, and here is his remarkable, prize-winning recipe, given me by Mrs. Breakstone. It is delicious to the point of sin.

What You Will Need

For the crust:	*For the cake:*
1 box zwieback	Four 3-ounce packages cream cheese
¼ pound melted butter	(room temperature)
1 cup sugar	6 eggs
¼ tsp. cinnamon	1¼ cups sugar
A 9″ springform	rind of ½ lemon
	1 tbsp. vanilla
	¼ cup flour
	1 quart sour cream

1. Preheat the oven to 325F. Crush the zwieback with a rolling pin and mix it together in a bowl with the melted butter, the cinnamon, and 1 cup of sugar.

2. Set aside ½ cup of the zwieback mixture. With the rest, form a crust on the bottom and halfway up the sides of the greased springform. Pat the crumbs firmly against the springform with the heels of your hands.

3. Set the crust aside and in a new mixing bowl blend together the cream cheese and the sugar.

4. Separate the egg yolk from the whites, gradually mixing the yolks into the cheese and sugar mixture, and slipping the whites into a clean bowl, where they will later be whipped until stiff.

5. Grate the rind of ½ lemon and fold it gently into the egg yolk, cheese, and sugar mixture. Then fold in 1 tablespoon of vanilla extract, ¼ cup of flour, and 1 quart of sour cream.

6. Whip the egg whites until they stand in peaks and gently fold them into the mixture.

7. Spoon the mixture into the springform and sprinkle the ½ cup of crushed zwieback, which you earlier set aside, over the top.

8. Bake for 1 hour and five minutes in a 325F oven. Then turn off the oven and leave the door closed for 1 hour. Then open the door and let the cheesecake sit in the oven, slowly and magnificently cooling, for

one more hour. This is a bothersome process, but patience is the principal ingredient of success.

9. Remove the cheesecake from the oven, let it cool until it has reached room temperature, and remove the sides of the springform.

NOTE: This recipe serves 12. The cheesecake keeps beautifully in the refrigerator for several days, but is best eaten fresh.

TYCOON CHEESE CAKE

What You Will Need

8 ounces of cream cheese warmed to room temperature	1 cup sugar
12 ounces of fine cottage cheese	1 cup heavy cream
5 eggs	2 tablespoons sugar
¼ teaspoon salt	1 tsp. vinegar
¾ teaspoon almond extract	½ tsp. vanilla
	shaved bitter chocolate

1. Beat the five eggs thoroughly with a fork and fold in the sugar.

2. Fold in the cottage cheese, the cream cheese, the almond extract, and the salt.

3. Beat well and pour into a buttered cake pan or two pie tins.

4. Bake 45 to 50 minutes at 325F or until set. Remove from the oven and cool on a rack for 20 minutes.

5. When the cake is cool, sour 1 cup of heavy cream by adding a teaspoon of vinegar to it.

6. Mix in 2 tablespoons of sugar and ½ teaspoon vanilla extract and spread this sauce over the cake.

7. Return to the oven and bake for an additional 10 minutes (also at 325F). Cool and chill.

8. Before serving, decorate the cheese cake with shaved bitter chocolate.

A Dinner for Summer

The Menu:

Tomato Vichyssoise
Cold Roast Beef
Baked Idaho Potatoes
Tossed Green Salad (or Hearts of Lettuce)
Fruit Ambrosia with Coconut Snowballs

The contributors: Mr. G. H. Beeby, British Titan Products Co., Ltd.; Mr. George J. Hecht, Parents' Magazine Enterprises, Inc.

TOMATO VICHYSSOISE

This refreshing and colorful first course can be made simply by opening a few cans of vichyssoise and mixing them with a few cans of tomato juice and floating a sliced cucumber on top. But with just a little preparation you can make your own soup from scratch, as it were. The extra effort doubles the rewards.

What You Will Need

2 cups mashed potatoes	3 cups tomato juice
3 cups of milk	1 dash tabasco sauce
1 cup heavy cream	1 cup peeled and thinly sliced
¼ cup minced green onion	cucumbers

1. Boil and mash enough potatoes to fill two measuring cups (or use one package of instant mashed potatoes) and set them aside.

2. In a large saucepan saute the onions in a little of the tomato juice for 2 minutes.

3. Add the potatoes, milk, and cream to the onion and heat in the saucepan until hot but not boiling (180 degrees F). Be careful to avoid scalding the milk.

4. Stir in the tomato juice and the tabasco, cool, and chill.

5. Just before serving, float the cucumber slices on top.

NOTE: Tomato Vichyssoise may be stored in the refrigerator for as long as a week. And it may be served hot.

COLD ROAST BEEF

Mr. G. H. Beeby is Chairman of the Board of British Titan Products Co. Ltd. of England. His favorite dish is a standing rib roast, served cold and sliced wafer thin, and accompanied by an Idaho potato, baked and served in its skin with butter or a sour cream and chive filling, and with a lettuce heart salad and dressing. Mr. Beeby suggests claret or burgundy for the wine, or, and especially in the summer, the strong, dark English beer known as "stout." If stout is a bit strong for your taste, try mixing it with an ordinary light beer — half and half, or just add a few drops of the stout to a glass of ordinary beer for color and flavor. Stout mixed with champagne (half and half) is known as "Black Velvet" and was the favorite drink and the invention of Edward VII. It is extraordinarily fattening, must be accompanied by Strasbourg Paté de Fois Gras, and should be drunk only aboard a yacht.

If you intend to serve the roast cold you might prepare it a day in advance — or certainly quite early in the morning. Always remember that the roast will continue to cook slowly for about an hour after you have taken it out of the oven.

What You Will Need

8-pound standing rib roast, nicely marbled	1 roll of masking tape

1. Trim excess fat from the roast and let the roast warm to room temperature.

2. Preheat the oven to 425F.

3. Place the roast in the oven and tape the oven door closed with masking tape to seal in the heat and to prevent peekers. The door must not be opened.

4. Roast for one hour, turn the oven off, and let the roast remain in the oven for 4 hours. This slow roasting will produce a magnificently cooked roast, medium rare. When you open the oven the roast will still be very warm and may be eaten immediately. To serve it cold you must let it cool out of the oven for another hour or two and refrigerate it overnight.

NOTE: It is an English tradition to serve roast beef with hot mustard. If you cannot find a really hot mustard in your market, buy a can of dry mustard and dilute it with enough vinegar or water to make a creamy paste.

HEARTS OF LETTUCE

Mr. Beeby prefers a heart-of-lettuce salad to a tossed salad. This may present a few problems. Iceburg lettuce does not really have a heart — at least not one in the sense that Mr. Beeby means — namely, a heart that is young and gay, light, yellow, and spongy, and rather more tangy than the outer leaves. Boston lettuce does have such a heart, but the heart of the average head of Boston Lettuce is just enough for one man. If you are an altruist you will give it to him and eat the outer part yourself. But in this meal you are still left with four guests. So look over your budget and see how far you can go. Can you afford six heads of lettuce? Extravagance, after all, is the best revenge.

FRUIT AMBROSIA WITH COCONUT SNOWBALLS

Fruit Ambrosia is the favorite of Mr. George J. Hecht, Chairman of the Board of Parents' Magazine Enterprises Inc. The dessert, served in sherbet glasses, is a wondrous sight to behold and a dramatic way to end a summer dinner.

What You Will Need

6 oranges, peeled and petaled
2 cups pitted grapes
2 pears, peeled and sliced
3 bananas, sliced on the diagonal
2 tbsps. grenadine syrup
vanilla or rum flavoring

1 can pineapple chunks
½ pint heavy cream
2 tbsps. powdered sugar
¼ tsp. vanilla extract
½ cup shredded coconut

1. Lightly mix the fruit together in a chilled bowl.

2. In another, smaller bowl mix the grenadine and the juice from the pineapple.

3. Add the juice and the chunks of pineapple to the large bowl and chill for at least two hours before serving.

4. To serve, top with "snowballs" of sweetened, vanilla or rum flavored whipped cream lightly sprinkled with coconut.

A Dinner Quickly Prepared

The Menu:

Crabmeat Cocktail
Breast of Chicken à la Harry
Rice Pilaff
Woody's Salad
Mint Mousse

The contributors: Mr. Woodrow Wirsig, Better Business Bureau of New York; Enrico and Sergio Mariotti, Harry's Bar, Florence, Italy.

CRABMEAT COCKTAIL

So often the most standard restaurant fare is received with surprise and applause when served in the home — probably because food *always* tates better at home.

The crabmeat cocktail is a case in point. One tends to gloss over it in a restaurant. But when it appears in your own dining room it will cause quite a stir.

What You Will Need

3 pints of fresh crab meat (or 3 large cans of crab)	dash of tobasco sauce
3 lemons	dash of barbecue sauce
½ cup mayonnaise	6 leaves of crisp, fresh lettuce
¼ cup tomato ketchup	crushed ice (optional)
	parsley sprigs

1. A crabmeat cocktail must look glamorous. The best way to serve it requires a special dish: a tall, stemmed crystal glass with a wide bowl into which the crushed ice is packed. A smaller bowl, holding the crabmeat, is then nested atop the crushed ice. If you do not have such recherché equipment simply serve the cocktail on lettuce leaves in champagne glasses, or whatever other fancy glasses you have.

2. Line whichever dish you are using with a bit of lettuce, scoop generous spoonfuls of crabmeat on top, spoon over a tablespoon of sauce (see below) and serve with lemon wedges and parsley sprigs.

3. If you are using canned crabmeat, clean it carefully to remove the fibers, freshen it up with a sprinkling of lemon juice, and chill it.

FOR THE COCKTAIL SAUCE:

1. Mix together the mayonnaise and the ketchup.

2. Add tabasco and barbecue sauce to taste.

BREAST OF CHICKEN A LA HARRY

Europe boasts many Harry's Bars: one is in Paris, one in Venice (Hemingway's favorite), and one in Florence. All of them have at one time or another been notoriously chic, and all of them have been criticized by the tourists for being "too American." Harry's Bar in Paris has been abandoned by the Americans and taken over by French businessmen — though the specialty there is still the hot dog.

Harry's Bar in Florence does not serve hot dogs. Its only concession to tourists is excellent food, warm and richly appointed decor, impeccable service, and a delightful canape that resembles a miniature toasted cheese sandwich with a slice of Italian ham nestled among the cheese.

The proprietor of Harry's Bar in Florence is Enrico Mariotti, a rare prince of a man. Although I have tried to avoid the recipes of restaurant tycoons in this book — that is a book in itself — I am proud to present Enrico's recipe here.

"Chicken a la Harry" is what the French call a "supreme," meaning that the meat of the breast is skinned and removed from the bone and poached in butter for a few minutes. For a really quick dinner it may be served on instant rice or toast. A fancier way to serve it is on Rice Pilaff, which takes a half hour. Enrico's recipe for Rice Pilaff is listed below.

What You Will Need

6 chicken breasts	1 cup milk
5 tbsps. butter	½ cup heavy cream
1 cup Marsala wine	salt and pepper to taste
2 tbsps. flour	

1. Remove the skin from the 6 breasts and then carefully cut the meat away from the bone. Boning the breast is a simple process and if you have not tried it before I urge you to try it now. All you need is a sharp, slender knife and a little patience.

2. Sprinkle the meat *lightly* with flour and quickly brown in 3 tablespoons frothing butter in a large frying pan. This will take 1 minute.

3. Sprinkle on the salt and pepper, add the Marsala wine, and simmer for 8 minutes. The chicken is now done. It requires no more cooking.

4. Remove the chicken from the pan, place it on a warm serving dish, and spread Enrico's sauce over the platter.

FOR THE SAUCE:

1. Melt two tablespoons of butter in a heavy saucepan; in a separate saucepan bring the milk to a boil.

2. Quickly blend in two tablespoons of flour and stir with a fork until you have a smooth paste.

3. Keep the paste over a flame, stirring constantly, until just a touch of brown appears (less than a minute).

4. Pour in the boiling milk, blend, and gradually add the cream and the stock. Season with salt and pepper to taste and cook slowly, stirring constantly, until the sauce is thick and velvety.

NOTE: the sauce may be made in advance and reheated while you are poaching the chicken breasts.

HOW TO MAKE HARRY'S RICE PILAFF

Rice Pilaff, or Pilau, is a fairly standard way of doing rice, and certainly the elegant way. It is more tender and much more tasty than instant rice, and more subtle than the spiced rices that are currently in vogue. If you are serving it with chicken, use a chicken stock. If you are serving it with fish, a fish stock. And with beef, a beef stock. Here is what you will need:

½ cup chopped onion
2 cups long grain rice
2 tbsps. butter

4 cups stock (beef, chicken, or fish)
salt and pepper to taste

1. Place the stock in a saucepan and bring it to a boil.

2. While the stock is heating saute the onions in a heavy 2-quart saucepan.

3. When the onions are golden pour in the rice, turn up the flame, and stir constantly for 1 or 2 minutes — until the rice has become partially transparent.

4. Pour on the boiling stock, reduce the heat to a low flame, cover the saucepan, and simmer the rice gently for 18 minutes. The rice should now be moderately dry. It is done if the top of the rice resembles the surface of the moon, and if, when you spoon a bit of the rice away from the side of the saucepan, you find that the liquid has cooked away.

5. Turn off the heat and let the rice sit for 10 minutes before serving. The rice, covered, will retain its heat for a good hour.

WOODY'S SALAD

Mr. Woodrow Wirsig, known among his friends as "Woody," has done many fascinating things in his life. He has been editor-in-chief of Look Magazine and Woman's Home Companion; like most of our tycoons, he has served on many distinguished committees and has received impressive awards for public service. He is now President and Chief Executive Officer of the Better Business Bureau of New York. His favorite dish is Chocolate Fudge, but I was unable to fit it into a menu, and so I have taken his second choice — a most imaginative salad of his own invention.

1 head of lettuce	¼ pound blue cheese
2 pkgs. mixed, frozen vegetables	1 tbsp. milk

1. Cook the frozen, mixed vegetables according to the instructions on the box, but omitting the butter. (Frozen mixed vegetables usually include at least baby lima beans, carrots, peas, and onions).

2. Drain, cool, and chill the vegetables.

3. Mix the blue cheese and the milk together with a fork. It should have the consistency of thick gravy. Add more milk if necessary.

4. Toss the vegetables, the lettuce, and the blue cheese together and serve.

MINT MOUSSE

If you have been afraid to try a mousse, here is your chance to prove your courage, for this recipe is really a sort of mock mousse. There are no egg yolks to curdle, no egg whites to beat stiff. The dish can be made in a few minutes.

What You Will Need

1 package lemon gelatin	1 cup heavy cream
1 package lime gelatin	2 cups boiling water
1 cup crème de menthe	

1. Dissolve the gelatin in 2 cups of boiling water.

2. Stir in the crème de menthe. This thick, green liqueur is available in varying qualities. The cheapest will do, but the better the mint, the better the mousse.

3. Cool and chill the mixture until it is nearly set.

4. Whip the cream until it stands in peaks.

5. With an egg beater or electric mixer whip the gelatin mixture until it is frothy.

6. Fold in the whipped cream, pour into sherbet glasses, and chill until set (about one hour). The mousse may be decorated with shaved chocolate or cherries.

A Spanish Dinner

The Menu:

Gazpacho
Pollo de Valencia
Braised Green Peppers
Sangria
Tossed Green Salad
Melon Con Helados

The contributors: Mr. Joseph F. Cullman III, Philip Morris Inc.; Mr. Henry O. Golightly, Henry Golightly & Co., Inc.

GAZPACHO

A Spanish dinner need not be a heavy, garlicky, greasy affair. Indeed it should not be. It should be tasty, colorful, and served very late at night.

The first course, Gazpacho, is the contribution of Mr. Joseph F. Cullman III, Chairman of the Board of Philip Morris Inc. It is one of the few good recipes for gazpacho that can be done without a blender.

What You Will Need

1 tbsp. olive oil	2 tsps. Spanish paprika
1 cucumber	¼ cup tarragon wine vinegar
2 onions	1½ cups tomato juice
2 garlic cloves	1 cup chicken broth
5 tomatoes	¼ tsp. basil
2 green peppers	¼ tsp. tarragon
1 stalk celery	

1. Peel the cucumber. Run the prongs of a fork down its sides to create a scalloped effect, slice it thinly, sprinkle with salt and vinegar, and chill.

2. Chop finely all of the remaining vegetables and mix them in a large bowl with the rest of the ingredients. (You may blenderize the vegetables if you like; the Spanish would not.)

NOTE: The tomatoes should be peeled and cored before chopping.

3. Chill the soup in the refrigerator for at least three hours before serving. It can be prepared in advance and stored in the refrigerator for days.

4. Garnish the soup with sliced cucumber and serve.

BRAISED GREEN PEPPERS

Here is an unusual way of preparing peppers. They may be served with any meal, and are especially good with Pollo de Valencia. Try to find fresh, large green peppers.

What You Will Need

6 large green peppers	2 tbsps. olive oil
1 yellow onion, thinly sliced	1 tsp. vinegar
(medium-size onion)	1 tbsp. butter

1. Remove the seeds and stems from the peppers and slice them into long strips a half inch wide.

2. Heat the oil and the butter in a skillet.

3. Add the peppers, onion, and vinegar and simmer slowly for fifteen minutes or until tender. Add more vinegar if necessary.

POLLO DE VALENCIA

Anyone who has been in Valencia during the orange season will understand why this recipe calls for oranges; the city is filled with them.

The oranges lend a delightful fragrance to the chicken and send forth, as they roast, an aroma that makes one think of spring and of flamenco dancers.

One suggestion: plunge the bacon into boiling water and simmer it for 6 to 7 minutes before draping it over the chicken. A strongly smoked bacon tends to steal flavor from chicken and oranges. This recipe is the favorite of Mr. Henry O. Golightly, President of Henry Golightly & Co. Inc. Mr. Golightly suggests saffron rice with the chicken. It will not be necessary for this menu, however.

What You Will Need

2 chickens cut into serving pieces	1 medium-size jar olives
4 large oranges	stuffed with pimientos
2 lemons	1 pound thick bacon
1 cup red wine	salt and pepper to taste

1. Coat the bottom of a casserole with a little red wine.

2. Slice the oranges and the lemons and place them on the bottom of the casserole.

3. Slice the olives and place them on top of the oranges and the lemons.

4. Salt and pepper the chicken and place it on top of the olives.

5. Completely cover the chicken with the bacon slices (preferably blanched bacon — see description, above).

6. Place the casserole in a 375F oven and cook for 50 minutes, basting sparingly with the red wine and juice from the bottom of the pan.

MELON CON HELADOS

Nothing could be simpler than this dessert, which is as popular in America as it is in Spain. You will need three ripe cantelope melons and one quart of vanilla ice cream.

Keep the melons at room temperature. When ready to serve, cut them in half, seed them, fill them with ice cream, and place them on the table.

SANGRIA

Sangria is a famous Spanish fruit wine — not a punch, really, but not entirely a wine. It should be served in wine glasses from a large, clear glass pitcher. It is a ravishing sight, and if your guests are wine drinkers you had better double the recipe below, for it vanishes with amazing speed.

What You Will Need

1 bottle dry red Spanish wine
One 8-ounce bottle soda water
2 oranges

1 lemon
6 maraschino cherries and their juice

1. Squeeze and strain the juice of one orange.
2. Mix the juice, the wine, and the soda together.
3. Slice and seed the remaining orange and the lemon.
4. Add the fruit slices and the cherries to the wine.
5. Chill, and add a few ice cubes to the Sangria when you serve it. This will keep it cold as it sits on the table and will not dilute the wine enough to harm its flavor.

NOTE: Do not serve the slices of fruit in the wine glasses. They are for appearance and flavor only, and are not to be eaten.

A Curry Dinner

The Menu:

Chicken Curry
Riz à l'Indienne
Chutney
Dahl
Sombol
Oranges Lebanese

The contributors: Mr. Howard Johnson, Howard Johnson Company; Mr. Walter Stace, ex-Mayor of Colombo; Mr. Raif Bakht, Arab Marketing & Finance Inc.

CHICKEN CURRY

When a letter from Howard Johnson arrived in my mailbox one morning not long ago, I opened it with anxious fingers, hoping that the secrets of the 28 flavors would at last be unfolded to me. They were not. But I was not disappointed, for after all, the ice cream may be bought easily enough. What I received instead was a recipe for chicken curry that is a classic. I was especially pleased because I had already received the recipes for the traditional accompaniments to a chicken curry — dahl and sombol — from a former mayor of Colombo, Ceylon. The next day's mail brought a dessert recipe from Lebanon, which added the final glory to a thoroughly Eastern meal.

Mr. Johnson's recipe for curry may be used for lamb, beef, shrimp, lobster, or any other meat you would like to curry.

What You Will Need

2 tbsps. butter	2 sprigs fresh thyme, finely chopped
2 three-pound chickens cut into	(or ⅓ tsp. dried thyme)
serving pieces	1 bay leaf
salt to taste	1 cup canned Italian plum tomatoes
½ cup finely chopped celery	1½ cups chicken broth
1 cup finely chopped onions	pepper to taste
¼ cup hot curry powder	1 cup heavy cream
2 cloves garlic, minced	¼ cup flour

1. Preheat the oven to 400F.

2. In a large, deep, and heavy casserole melt the butter.

3. Add the pieces of chicken. Simmer them for 5 minutes, stirring constantly. Do not brown the chicken.

4. Sprinkle the meat with salt and add celery and onion. Stir well and add curry powder. Do not brown the chicken.

5. Add the tomatoes, cover, and cook over a medium flame for 10 minutes. Sprinkle with flour and immediately stir all ingredients until well coated with flour.

6. Bring to a boil on the top of the stove. Cover the pot, put it into the oven, and bake for 45 minutes.

7. When the chicken is tender remove it to a large serving platter. Bring the broth in the casserole to a boil and cook over a moderately high heat for 10 minutes. Stir frequently, for the sauce might have a tendency to stick.

8. Add the cream and pepper to taste. Strain the sauce over the chicken and serve.

NOTE: Curried chicken may be prepared a day in advance and be reheated before serving. Curry experts believe that such advance cooking actually improves the flavor.

Curry is usually served with chutney, which I suggest you do not try to make yourself. The commercial brands are perfectly satisfactory.

DAHL AND SOMBOL

Dahl is a kind of pea soup and Sombol is a spicy, fluffy coconut relish. The two dishes are the traditional accompaniments to curry; Sombol stimulates the palate, Dahl cools the tongue. Both should be served in small portions, the Dahl warm, in consomme cups, the Sombol cold, on the plate with the curry.

These two recipes are the favorites of Professor Walter Stace, the distinguished philosopher who was a tycoon in 1920, when he was mayor of Colombo, Ceylon. If you have an opportunity to journey to Colombo you will find "Stace Street" — the only street left in that city which still bears an Englishman's name. The recipes were provided by Mr. Stace's wife, Blanche, whom he met in Ceylon many years ago.

What You Will Need for Dahl

1 can condensed pea soup	1½ cups chopped green pepper
1 can milk	1 tbsp. cinnamon
1½ cups chopped onions	

Mix the ingredients together and simmer them slowly, over water, for two hours. Dahl may be made as much as a week in advance and reheated upon serving.

I personally like to add a large can of fruit cocktail to the dahl. Mrs. Stace, however, who is the expert, is horrified at such prostitution of Ceylonese cuisine.

What You Will Need for Sombol

1 pound shredded coconut	1 tbsp. cayenne pepper
1 cup milk	½ cup finely chopped onion
¾ cup lemon juice	pinch of salt

1. Soak the shredded coconut in milk for one hour.

2. Drain the milk and add to the coconut the cayenne pepper, the lemon juice, the salt, and the onions.

3. Mix thoroughly and chill for at least one hour.

NOTE: Sombol may be prepared in advance and will keep in the refrigerator indefinitely.

RIZ A L'INDIENNE

In the East, curry is frequently served with "stringhoppers," which are long, thin strands of rice formed into little nest-like shapes. String-hoppers are extremely difficult to buy in Western lands, and Riz à l'Indienne — another contribution from Howard Johnson — make them unnecessary. This rice will receive as much praise as the curry itself.

What You Will Need

2 cups long grain rice
4 cups chicken broth
2 tbsps. butter

½ cup chopped onion
1 cup blanched raisins
1 cup blanched almonds
salt and pepper to taste

For the rice, follow the instructions for Harry's Rice Pilaff in Chapter X. When the rice is done, fold in the raisins and the almonds. Serve with the curried chicken.

ORANGES LEBANESE

This recipe has the triple advantage of being exotic, simple, and light. It may be prepared in the morning, set aside, and not touched until it is time to serve. Oranges Lebanese is the favorite of Mr. Raif Bakht, President of Arab Marketing & Finance, Inc., of Beirut, Lebanon. In Lebanon the dish is served warm. Westerners generally seem to prefer it chilled.

What You Will Need

6 large, juicy oranges
¼ cup almonds
¾ cup honey
¾ cup water

1 teaspoon cinnamon
2 tbsps. brown sugar
1 cup dried rose petals (optional)
2 cups fine cottage cheese

1. Peel one of the oranges thinly and carefully. With a spoon or sharp knife scrape off all of the white pith and fibers.

2. Slice the peels into tiny, thin slivers, an inch or two long. Cook them slowly in the water and honey, and, if you are able to get them, the rose petals. You may use a few fresh rose petals if you like.

3. When the peelings are cooked (they will be translucent when done) remove the pan from the stove.

4. Peel the remaining oranges and petal them. Take care to remove every trace of the white pith, and all seeds.

5. Add the orange slices to the cooked peel and its syrup and heat until the oranges are warmed through.

6. Sprinkle crisp toasted almonds atop the oranges and set aside (chill if you like).

7. Serve on dessert plates with generous portions of chilled cottage cheese (which is a fair substitute for a Middle-Eastern dish known as *kaimak*).

A Russian Dinner

The Menu:

Caviar Mold

Borschok

Pirojkis

Shashlik Caucasian

Russian Charlotte

The contributors: Mr. Ely R. Callaway, Jr., Burlington Industries; Col. Serge Obolensky, Serge Obolensky Associates, Inc.

CAVIAR MOLD

A dinner in the Russian style requires high spirits, fortitude, romantic music, and serious drinking. There must be caviar, and it must be served with an endless supply of chilled vodka, drunk quickly and with courage.

A small amount of caviar may be stretched to serve quite a few people with this recipe from Ely Callaway, President of Burlington Industries. The recipe calls for pasteurized caviar, but fresh caviar may be used. Fresh caviar, however, is hard to find except in large metropolitan areas, and is so delicious and expensive that it really should be served without embellishments. If you are reluctant to use endless supplies of vodka, you may substitute dry champagne. Whichever drink you use, serve it throughout the dinner. The Caviar Mold is time consuming but is a beautiful sight to behold, and may be made several days in advance and stored in the refrigerator.

What You Will Need

a 3-cup ring mold (preferably metal)
8 oz. jar pasteurized Beluga caviar
3-4 white pearl onions,
   finely minced
3-4 chopped, hard-cooked egg yolks

1½ envelopes unflavored gelatin
2 cups fish stock or clam juice
12 lemon wedges
1 cup cultured sour cream
½ cup parsley

1. Place 2 cups of the fish stock into an enamel or stainless steel saucepan and heat until just lukewarm. Remove from heat. (NOTE: Mr. Callaway's recipe for fish stock appears below; if this seems too much trouble for you, substitute 2 cups of clam juice.)

2. Place the caviar in a strainer, and dip and swirl it gently around in the stock.

3. Clarify the stock. This is done by adding a slightly beaten egg white and its crushed shell to the stock. Heat the stock slowly, stirring constantly with a wire whip until the stock is simmering. Move the saucepan gently to one side of the heat so that one edge of the liquid is barely bubbling. Rotate the saucepan a quarter turn every five minutes for 15 minutes. Then line a very clean sieve or colander with 5 layers of well washed, damp cheesecloth, and very gently ladle the stock and egg white mixture into the cheesecloth. Be careful to make sure that the bottom of the sieve remains above the surface of the liquid which has already passed through.

4. Now the stock is clarified. Let it cool and sprinkle 1½ envelopes of unflavored gelatin (about 1½ tablespoons) into ⅓ cup of the cold stock and allow it to soften for 5 minutes.

5. Add the softened gelatin to the clarified stock and bring just to the boil, stirring constantly until all the gelatin particles have dissolved.

6. Chill the stock over a bowl of cracked ice until the mixture is syrupy and almost set.

7. Pour the almost-set jelly into the mold and place the mold in the bowl of cracked ice. As soon as ⅛ an inch layer of the jellied stock has set around the edges of the mold, pour out the unset jelly. If too thick a layer has formed in the bottom of the mold, dip a spoon in hot water and scoop it out.

8. Chill the mold for about 15 minutes until the jellied stock lining is stiff. Then add the caviar to the mold and cover with a thin layer of the unset (but not liquid) jelly, and chill again.

9. Add the minced onion, then another layer of the jellied stock, and chill once more until set. Then add the chopped egg yolks, finishing with a thin layer of the jelly.

10. Cover the mold and chill it in the refrigerator until set — a good three hours.

11. To serve Caviar Mold, you must unmold it. This is done by dipping the mold into hot water for 3 or 4 seconds, inverting a chilled serving platter over the top of the mold, and turning the mold upside down. Give a sharp downward thrust to transfer the caviar from its mold to the platter.

12. Garnish with parsley and lemon wedges and fill the center of the ring with sour cream. Serve with thinly sliced pieces of fresh toast.

FOR THE STOCK

If you have the time and the energy you will want to make your own stock. For this you will need:

A 6-8 quart kettle	1 stalk celery with leaves
2 lbs. fresh fish, fish heads, bones, trimmings	1 bay leaf
	½ tsp. thyme
2 onions, thinly sliced	6-8 parsley stems
4 peppercorns	2 tsps. lemon juice
1 large carrot, scraped and sliced in half, lengthwise	¼ tsp. salt
	1½ cups dry white wine
	cold water to cover the ingredients

1. Place all of the ingredients in the kettle.

2. Bring to a simmer, and simmer uncovered for 30-45 minutes.

3. Strain through a sieve lined with cheesecloth.

The stock may be frozen and defrosted when needed, or it may be refrigerated. If it is to be refrigerated, bring it to a boil every 2 days to keep it from spoiling.

BORSCHOK

The recipes for Borschok, Pirojkis, and Shashlik Caucasian all come from Col. Obolensky, President of Serge Obolensky Associates, Inc., and famous New York "man-about-town." Col. Obolensky acquired these recipes from one of the great Russian chefs, Basil Yourchenko, who was educated in Grand Duke Vladimar's kitchen under the tutelege of the best French chefs of the time. Yourchenko fled Russia with the Obolensky family and stayed in the service of Serge's wife, Alice Astor, until her death.

What You Will Need

1 gallon beef stock	1 pound of onions, sliced
2 pounds raw beets, sliced	½ cup madeira wine
1 tbsp. salt	1 bunch fresh parsley
½ cup vinegar	2 tbsps. sugar

1. Combine the beef stock, the beets, the onions, and the parsley in an 8-quart kettle and cook slowly for 1 hour.

2. Add the vinegar, salt, and sugar, and bring the soup back to a rapid boil.

3. Strain the soup through cheese cloth.

4. Just before serving, add ½ glass of madeira wine.

NOTE: This recipe serves 10. Borschok may be stored in the refrigerator for several days.

PIROJKIS

Pirojkis are superb as appetizers with cocktails for any dinner. For the Russian Dinner, however, we are having caviar with our vodka, and will serve the Pirojkis with the soup.

What You Will Need

2¼ cups sifted, all purpose flour	1 tbsp. sugar
½ cup warm milk	2 eggs
1 cake of yeast	½ pound ground beef
½ cup of butter	salt & pepper to taste

1. Mix the yeast and the warm milk together and let them ferment for 10 minutes.

2. Mix the flour and butter together until evenly balanced.

3. Beat the eggs gently and add them to the flour and butter.

4. Blend in the yeast, milk, and sugar. Cover the bowl with a clean dish towel and set it aside in a warm place for 20 minutes.

5. While the dough is rising, sauté the ground beef until it is light brown in color, and season it with salt and pepper. Set it aside.

5. Punch down the dough and roll it out to a thickness of ⅛ of an inch. Cut it into small, round pieces.

7. Place a teaspoon of the ground beef in the center of patty, fold the dough over, and form small balls.

8. Line a cookie sheet with waxed paper, arrange the pirojkis on it, and bake for 25 minutes at 350F. Serve them hot.

SHASHLIK CAUCASIAN

This dish must be started three or four days before it is to be served to give the lamb proper time to marinate. But don't let the time element discourage you, for once the marinating process has been completed there is very little else to do, and if you have a hibachi burner or a charcoal grill your guests can help you. By this time, having been drinking vodka or champagne steadily, they will need the exercise.

What You Will Need

A 5-pound leg of lamb	1 cup olive oil
2 large onions	1 tbsp. salt
2 green peppers	4 peppercorns, ground
2 lemons	Cooked rice, to serve 6
1 bottle Sauce Diable	¼ cup chopped parsley

1. Cut the raw meat from the leg of lamb into 1″ cubes, removing all of the fat.

2. Chop the onions and green peppers into quarters.

3. Mix together the lamb cubes, the onions and green peppers, the

parsley, the olive oil, and the salt and pepper. Marinate them in the refrigerator for three or four days.

4. When you are ready to eat, spear the cubes of lamb on skewers and broil over charcoal (or in your oven) for 15 minutes.

5. Serve the shashlik on a bed of rice and season with Sauce Diable, which is similar to Escoffier Sauce. A-1 Sauce may be substituted if you cannot find Sauce Diable in your market.

RUSSIAN CHARLOTTE

The Charlotte is a dessert made in a charlotte mold or a souffle dish. A Charlotte russe is a dessert made by lining the mold with lady fingers and pouring in a Bavarian cream — similar to the recipe for Glen Cove Cream, found in the chapter of this book called "A Barbequed Dinner." If you want to serve an authentic Charlotte russe for this dinner, you might serve Glen Cove Cream as your dessert and proclaim it to be "Charlotte Malakoff au Chocolat."

But you might prefer to serve a straightforward Russian Charlotte — a dessert of my own invention. The Russian dinner we have read about so far in this chapter requires considerable preparation and is fairly rich. Even if you have the time to prepare an authentic Charlotte, your guests might not appreciate it after such a meal.

And so I present the Russian Charlotte, which is simple and dramatic — and drama is needed for dessert, in the grand Russian tradition. Ice cream, incidentally, is a favorite dessert of Russians.

What You Will Need

12 lady fingers
1 cup Cherry Heering
1 pint coffee ice cream

1 pint strawberry sherbet
1 pint lemon ice
½ cup minted cherries

1. Sprinkle Cherry Heering liberally over the lady fingers until they are nicely flavored and reddish (the modern Russia) but not so saturated that they crumble.

2. Line the lady fingers in a 2-quart Charlotte mold or souffle dish. The lady fingers at the bottom of the dish may be placed either spiral or sunburst fashion; the lady fingers on the side should stand straight up.

3. With an ice cream scoop, ladle the coffee ice cream into the mold. Sprinkle on a few minted cherries.

4. Scoop on the Strawberry sherbet, and again sprinkle a few minted cherries around.

5. Scoop on the lemon ice, and sprinkle on any remaining cherries or Cherry Heering. Cover the mold with aluminum foil and place in your freezer for at least 2 hours before serving.

6. To serve, unmold in the kitchen and carry to the table. For extra interest the unmolded Charlotte may be decorated with maraschino cherries and garnished with a half cup of Cherry Heering dribbled liberally over the mold.

A Mexican Fiesta

The Menu:

Cactus Soup Acapulco
Tacos De Luxe
Green Enchilada
Guacamole
Natilla

The contributors: Mr. Victor Bergeron, Trader Vic's; Mr. G. M. Metcalf, Sears, Roebuck and Co.

CACTUS SOUP ACAPULCO

Mexico has always been in, but right now it is more in than ever. All of the rich and beautiful people — the children of tycoons — have descended on it, abandoning the older playgrounds of Palm Beach, Capri, Monte Carlo. And they have been pleasantly surprised, for not only is the scenery breathtaking, the weather kind, the culture ancient, the cities picturesque. The food, too, is unique, distinctly Mexican.

So let us begin the fiesta with a nice little soup made from baby cactus, which may be purchased in cans at most Mexican or Spanish stores. If you cannot find it, substitute green pepper, which is similar in taste and appearance, if rather dull of name.

What You Will Need

2 cups chopped baby cactus	2 cups whole tomatoes, peeled and
2 cups beef broth	cored
1 cup dry white wine	1 cup cooked chick peas

Combine the ingredients, bring to a boil, and serve hot or cold. Either way is fine. Canned chick peas are ideal for this soup, incidentally, and need no pre-cooking.

TACOS DE LUXE

Tortillas — pronounced "tor-*teeh*-ha" — are flat, round pastry that resemble papahdums or pancakes. They are generally made from a corn flour and today may be purchased, frozen, in most supermarkets.

When tortillas are fried crisp and golden and served with a sauce they are called tacos — pronounced "*tah*-kos." When they are fried just until soft, then stuffed or rolled, they are called enchilada — pronounced "uhn-chill-*ah*-da." And when they are fried crisp and crumbled up into bits the result is tostadas, pronounced as written. For this fiesta we will have tortillas in all three forms.

Tacos De Luxe comes from Mr. Gordon M. Metcalf, Chairman of the Board of Sears, Roebuck & Co. He brought the recipe back from Mexico recently, and it is a favorite of both Mr. Metcalf and his wife.

What You Will Need

6 large tortillas	1 tsp. chili powder
3 lbs. ground beef	salt and pepper to taste
2 large onions, chopped	1 tbsp. paprika
3 small cans tomato & green chili sauce	*For the Salad:*
1 can refried beans	3 green onions, chopped
1 cup grated cheddar cheese	12 ripe olives, chopped
2 avocado, peeled and sliced	2 cubed tomatoes
1 cup sour cream	3 tbsps. tomato & green chili sauce

1. Make the salad, by mixing the green onions, the ripe olives, the cubed tomatoes, and the tomato and green chili sauce in a salad bowl. Store it in the refrigerator until 30 minutes before you are ready to serve the Tacos De Luxe.

2. Fry the tortillas — flat — until golden and crisp. This may be done a day or two before you use them. They will keep well, without refrigeration, in a brown paper bag.

3. Sauté the chopped onion until it is golden.

4. Add the ground beef, and sauté until the meat is light brown, but pink on the inside.

5. Drain off any fat that may have accumulated and add all but about 3 tablespoons of the tomato and green chili sauce.

6. Stir, and add the paprika, chili powder, and salt and pepper to taste. Simmer gently for 30 minutes, stirring occasionally.

8. To serve:

    A. On each plate place one taco.

    B. Over the taco spoon a layer of the hot meat mixture

    C. Over the meat mixture spoon a layer of hot, refried beans.

    D. Over the beans sprinkle a layer of grated cheese.

    E. Over the cheese add equal portions of the salad.

    F. Over the salad arrange a few slices of avocado.

    G. Crown each dish with a tiara of sour cream.

GREEN ENCHILADA

Mexican cooking, in fact, is so fascinating and diverse, that more than one tycoon has become enchanted with it, and after serving your first Mexican dinner your guests will hound you for a repeat performance. Surprise them, then, with a meal that is equally Mexican, but utterly different. Use the same first course and the same dessert, but for the main course give them Green Enchilada and, as a salad, Guacamole. The recipe for Green Enchilada comes from Victor Bergeron, also known as Trader Vic. Anyone who has been fortunate enough to visit one of the famous Trader Vic's restaurants needs no further encouragement to try this recipe. (Trader Vic's personal guide to vintage California wines appears elsewhere in this book.)

What You Will Need

For the Green Sauce:

2 cans cream of mushroom soup	½ cup raw pureed spinach
1 small can Ortega chilies (3½ oz.)	½ tsp. salt
1 large onion, chopped	½ tsp. monosodium glutamate
1 clove garlic, minced	2 tbsps. flour
1 can chicken broth	½ pint sour cream

1. Puree the mushroom soup, the chilies, the onions, and the garlic in a blender.

2. Add the blended mixture to the chicken broth and bring to a boil.

3. Add the pureed spinach and seasonings and simmer for 10 minutes.

4. Thicken the sauce with flour mixed with a little cold water. Stir the flour into the sauce a bit at a time and bring to a boil. Reduce the heat and stir constantly to avoid lumping.

5. Set the sauce aside and prepare the enchilada.

For the Enchilada:

2 cups cottage cheese
1 pound white cheddar cheese, grated
¼ cup chopped cooked onions
¼ cup crushed tostadas
   (made with 2 tortillas)
2 tbsps. chopped ripe olives
2 tbsps. chopped jalapeno chilies
1 tsp. salt
1 tsp. pepper
1 tsp. monosodium glutamate
12 tortillas

1. Fry 2 tortillas in oil until crisp. Remove them from the pan and crush them.

2. Mix the crushed tortillas (tostadas) together with the cottage cheese and the cheddar, the onions, the olives, and the chilies.

3. Add the seasonings and set the mixture aside.

4. Fry the 12 tortillas in oil until they are soft and pliable, but not crisp.

5. Drain the tortillas and dip them into the green sauce, coating both sides completely.

6. Spoon the cheese filling into the center of the tortillas and roll them.

7. Arrange the rolled, stuffed tortillas on a greased baking dish with the overlapping edges down.

8. Pour the remaining green sauce over the rolled cheese enchiladas and bake them in a 350° oven for 20 minutes.

9. Remove them from the oven, top with sour cream, and serve.

GUACAMOLE

Mr. Metcalf's recipe — Tacos De Luxe — is really a meal in itself. The cactus soup will whet the appetite, the dessert will sweeten the soul. Trader Vic's Green Enchilada, having no salad tossed on top of it, goes very nicely with Guacamole, a fresh vegetable salad made primarily from avocados. There are many variations on Guacamole. This one is simple and delicious.

What You Will Need

6 ripe avocados	¼ cup lemon juice
1 tomato	2 tbsps. capers
1 tsp. salt	2 tbsps. cognac

1. Peel and core the avocados. Spoon the meat into a blender.

2. Peel and core the tomatoes and add to the avocados.

3. Add the remaining ingredients, blend until evenly mixed, and serve on salad plates. If you do not have a blender, you may mash the ingredients together with a fork.

NATILLA

Here is a light, simple, refreshing Mexican dessert. I wrested the recipe from Roberto Osorio, Chef at the Hacienda La Paloma, a New York City restaurant that is a meeting place for many Mexophile tycoons.

What You Will Need

4 cups milk	3 tbsps. cognac
6 egg yolks	¼ cup mashed banana
1 cup sugar	1 tbsp. shredded coconut
2 tbsps. corn starch	1 tsp. vanilla flavoring

1. Scald 3 cups of milk and add the coconut. Set it aside.

2. In a mixing bowl, beat the egg yolks and the sugar until the mixture forms a thin thread. Then gradually add the cornstarch, the vanilla, the cognac, the mashed banana, and 1 cup of cold milk.

3. When you have thoroughly mixed the ingredients included in step 2, add them slowly to the scalded milk, stirring with a wire whip.

4. Heat the mixture, stirring constantly, until it begins to thicken.

5. Pour the natilla into champagne glasses, and sprinkle with cinnamon, if desired. Serve warm or cold.

A Creole Dinner

The Menu:
Madrilene Creole
Crab Gumbo
Crème Brûlée

The contributors: Mr. Harold L. Bache, Bache & Co.; Mrs. Letitia Baldrige, Letitia Baldrige Enterprises.

MADRILENE CREOLE

Creole — the word can mean so many things. Webster defines it as a person of French or Spanish descent born and reared in a colonial or remote region, especially the tropics. But that is only the first definition. There are many more. For cooking purposes, Larousse Gastronomique defines it as a term applying to dishes that contain a rice garnish complemented by sweet peppers simmered in a little oil and tomatoes.

For Americans, "Creole" usually means New Orleans — and food that is part French, part Spanish, part Indian, but mostly a wonderful time. For if Creole means New Orleans, New Orleans means Mardi Gras. If you can't get to New Orleans for Mardi Gras, you can bring New Orleans to you with this festive menu.

What You Will Need

3 cans jellied tomato madrilene	1 can whole kernel corn, drained
1 cup chopped sweet peppers	¼ cup chopped pimientos

1. Mix the ingredients together in a saucepan, bring to a boil, and simmer for 10 minutes.

2. To serve hot, pour the soup into soup bowls and top with cultured sour cream.

3. To serve cold, let the soup cool, pour it into a bowl, and place it in the refrigerator until it has jelled. Just before serving add ¼ cup dry sherry, whip it up with a wire whisk until frothy, and scoop it into consomme cups or sherbet glasses. Top with sour cream and garnish with parsley.

CRAB GUMBO

This recipe comes from Harold L. Bache, Chairman of the Board of Bache & Co. It is one that Mr. Bache prepared himself, and described as "the most sought after and famous in the Bache dietary program."

What You Will Need

2 lbs. okra—fresh or frozen	3 quarts chicken stock
2 chopped green peppers	6 bay leaves
1 chopped onion	1 tsp. thyme
4 tbsps. oil	1 lb. crab meat
1 large can tomatoes	1 tbsp. file powder*
2 lbs. fresh shrimp	2 tsps. salt
1 cup diced, cooked ham	1 tsp. pepper
¼ cup chopped parsley	Cooked rice to serve 6

*Gumbo File is an herb difficult to obtain. If you cannot find it substitute 1 tsp. saffron or simply omit it.

1. Place the fresh okra, the green peppers, and the onions in melted fat in an iron soup kettle. Simmer for 10 minutes. If you are using frozen okra, add it to the Gumbo 15 minutes before serving.

2. Add the tomatoes and simmer for 15 minutes.

3. Add the deveined raw shrimp and simmer another 10 minutes.

4. Add the diced cooked ham, the stock, bay leaves, thyme, salt, pepper, and crabmeat. Simmer very slowly in a covered kettle for 1 hour.

5. Sprinkle in the file powder or saffron.

6. To serve, ladle the Gumbo over generous portions of rice and garnish with parsley.

CREME BRULEE

Letitia Baldrige Hollensteiner, after a distinguished diplomatic career — which included serving as Mrs. John F. Kennedy's press secretary during the JFK administration — turned fairly recently to the world of commerce and, to no one's surprise, rose quickly to the top, like the very rich cream you must use in her favorite recipe for Crème Brûlée.

Crème Brûlée, long a specialty of New Orleans, gained particular prominence when President Kennedy announced it his favorite dessert. Miss Baldrige did not get this recipe from him, however. It came from Mrs. Dean Witter, whose husband's favorite recipe appears elsewhere in this book (see the index of tycoons).

Tish, who now heads up her own company in Chicago — Letitia Baldrige Enterprises — cautions readers that this recipe is for non-dieters only.

What You Will Need

4 egg yolks	2 cups heavy cream
1 pan hot water	6 tbsps. brandy
2 tbsps. brown sugar	3 tbsps. brown sugar

1. Heat 2 cups heavy cream in the top of a double boiler until warm. Stir it constantly and don't let it boil.

2. Stir in 3 tablespoons of brown sugar and 3 tablespoons of good brandy.

3. Beat 4 egg yolks and stir into the cream. Pour into a pyrex dish (about 8 inches in diameter).

4. Place the dish in a pan of hot water in a 250°F oven and bake for 1 hour and 10 minutes.

5. Remove from the oven to cool: then place in the refrigerator and chill thoroughly. *All this should be done the night before the party.*

6. The morning of the party, cover the surface of the pudding with a layer of sifted brown sugar.

7. Place under a hot broiler for a few seconds — until the sugar has carmelized.

8. Cover the dish with foil and return to the refrigerator until time to serve. Just before serving, splash the remaining brandy on top of the crust for extra zing.

A Dieter's Dream

The Menu:

Yoghurt Soup
Lo-Cal Roast Duckling
Whitehead Salad
Orange Cups

The contributors: Mr. John Elliott Jr., Ogilvy & Mather; Commander
Edward Whitehead, Schweppes (USA) Ltd.

YOGHURT SOUP

What is the dieter's dream? To lose weight without dieting. Tycoons, despite their busy lives, face, like everyone else enamoured of good food, the problem of restricting its intake. For the tycoon the problem of watching weight is intensified. He must stay slender not for appearances's sake or vanity, but to retain his health and energy. Yet he is constantly tempted by the great restaurants and chefs of the world. Such is his fate, and this is a menu to soothe his pain.

What You Will Need

3 cups "plain" yoghurt	1 cup diced cucumber
1 cup clam juice	1 tbsp. cointreau
¼ cup lemon juice	1 sprig fresh dill

1. Mix the yoghurt, clam and lemon juice, cucumbers, and cointreau together.

2. Pour the soup into consomme cups, decorate with sprigs of dill (parsley may be substituted if dill is out of season) and serve cold. A light sprinkling of paprika may be added on top of each serving for color, if desired.

LO-CAL ROAST DUCKLING

Duckling is the last thing one thinks of for dieters, but this way of cooking it removes every smidgen of fat, leaving a crisp skin and delicious meat. It is not for people who are fond of fatty meat, and was contributed by the wife of John Elliott Jr., who is Chairman of the Board of Ogilvy & Mather. Ogilvy & Mather is an advertising agency whose accounts include Schweppes, whose Chairman, Commander Whitehead, contributed the salad dressing for this menu.

What You Will Need

3 Long Island ducklings	salt & pepper to taste
3 onions	a sharp fork
3 tbsps. rosemary	a poultry shears
6 cloves	

1. If you are using frozen ducklings, which are fine, let them thaw slowly in the sink.

2. Two hours before serving, preheat the oven to 350°F.

3. Inside each duck insert one medium size, peeled onion into which you have pressed 2 cloves.

4. Place the ducks on a rack in a roasting pan, breast side up. Prick the skin of the breast with a fork.

5. Sprinkle salt and pepper liberally over the duck and then sprinkle onto each duck 1 tablespoon of rosemary.

6. Place the ducks in the oven. They must cook for 1¾ to 2 hours, and every 20 minutes you must prick the skin with the fork to let the fat run out. Halfway through this process you may find it necessary to remove with a bulb baster the fat that has accumulated at the bottom of the roasting pan.

7. When the skin is crisp and brown, remove the ducks and cut each in half with a poultry shears.

8. Serve with chilled applesauce lavishly spiced with nutmeg and cinnamon (canned applesauce is easily disguised this way).

As an accompaniment, Mrs. Elliott recommends a dark green salad with a lemony dressing. Therefore:

WHITEHEAD SALAD

Commander Edward Whitehead, Chairman of the Board of Schweppes (USA) Ltd. has achieved considerable fame for a variety of reasons. When a tycoon is in such excellent physical shape that he can personally advertise his own tonics, you can be sure that he is following a good diet. His favorite recipe is now known in several great restaurants as "The Whitehead Dressing." He would not commit himself to precise quantities, but if you follow these instructions you will have a healthful, slimming, and delicious salad.

What You Will Need

½ pound fresh spinach
½ cup chopped parsley
2 cups fresh watercress
1 lemon

1 tsp. minced garlic
6 tbsps. safflower oil
1 tsp. salt

1. Wash the spinach in cold water. Tear off the stems and discard them. Drain and dry.

2. Wash the watercress thoroughly in cold water and mix it together in a large bowl with the spinach and the parsley.

3. Wrap the green vegetables in a clean towel or in heavy paper towels and store in the refrigerator until ready to serve.

4. Squeeze the juice of one lemon into a mortar or a small sturdy bowl and crush the salt and the garlic into it with a pestal or the handle of a thick-handled knife.

5. When you are ready to serve the salad, place the vegetables in a large salad bowl and toss them with the safflower oil until all of the leaves are coated. (Any oil may be used here, but a polyunsaturated one — safflower, peanut, corn, etc. — is best for the diet conscious.)

6. When the leaves of the vegetables are well coated with oil, add the lemon juice, garlic, and salt mixture, and toss again.

7. Serve the salad with the duck or as a third course.

ORANGE CUPS

How can you serve a dessert that tastes rich and filling and sweet and is still low in calories? It's not easy. This dessert is not the sweetest, richest, or most filling dessert that has come along, but it is lovely to look at, delightful to taste, and heaven to lose weight by.

What You Will Need

6 large oranges
1 cup cottage cheese
¼ cup cognac

1½ cups strawberries
1 cup crushed pineapple

1. Select the largest, prettiest oranges you can find.

2. Slice the tops of the orange off with a sharp knife and hollow them with a spoon. This is a task that takes a little time (2 minutes for each orange) but is quite easy. Just remember that what you are trying to do is get all of the fruit out of the orange, but leave the shell of the orange intact.

3. Drain the juice from the can of crushed pineapple. Rinse it around each orange cup so that it coats the white pulp of the inside. Allow a few drops of the pineapple juice to remain at the bottom of each orange cup.

4. Spoon a heaping tablespoon of cottage cheese into each orange cup, packing it firmly with the backside of the spoon.

5. Pour ¼ cup cognac into a bowl and place the best six strawberries into it. Turn them over from time to time to absorb the cognac.

6. Place the rest of the strawberries in a bowl and mash them with a fork. Then spoon a layer of this over the cottage cheese layer that now rests at the bottom of the orange cup.

7. Add another layer of cottage cheese.

8. Add a layer of the crushed pineapple.

9. Continue this process — a layer of cottage cheese, then crushed strawberries, then cottage cheese, then crushed pineapple — until you reach the top of the orange shell. The quantities and numbers of layers obviously will vary according to the size of the orange. But finish with a sprinkling of cottage cheese.

10. Top each orange with one cognac-soaked strawberry. Place in the freezer one hour before serving.

11. The orange petals that have been removed from the oranges may be stored in the refrigerator and served for breakfast the following morning.

A Dinner for Royalty
The Menu:
Shad Roe Monogram
St. Germain Soup
Crown Roast of Lamb Petite
Brandied Peaches
Minted Pears
Braised Eggplant
Chocolate Souffle

The contributors: Mr. Andrew Goodman, Bergdorf Goodman; Mr. R. S. Bell, Packard Bell; Mr. Robert Murphy, Corning Glass; Mr. Gardner Cowles, Cowles Communications, Inc.

SHAD ROE MONOGRAM

Every so often a tycoon has a chance to entertain a king. And every so often a king has a chance to entertain a tycoon. Such dinners happen infrequently only because there are so few kings these days.

The tycoon, of course, is the modern version of royalty — he heads an empire of his own, and to keep it he must retain the patriotism and capture the imagination of hundreds of thousands of people, not only his employees, but all of the people who buy the products he manufactures.

Not all of us have frequent opportunities to entertain kings or tycoons. But we all, from time to time, are faced with the prospect of entertaining a group of people we hold higher, in our own esteem, than any others, a group of people we want to treat and feed as if they were royalty. So flatter them. Give them a meal they will remember forever.

What better way to start than with a monogram, if a coat of arms is lacking? This recipe comes from Andrew Goodman, President of Bergdorf Goodman, one of the most exclusive stores in New York, and one that has dressed and perfumed the wives of many a royal personage. It is a dish which his family cook invented, and is called "Monogram" because once, when his mother gave the recipe to a friend, she wrote it on monogram stationery. The name stuck.

What You Will Need

1 large shad roe	2 large egg yolks
2 tbsps. butter	3 egg whites
1 tbsp. flour	salt and pepper to taste
1 cup heavy cream	¼ cup lemon juice

1. Wash the roe carefully in cold, fresh water and gently separate the eggs with a silver fork.

2. In a heavy saucepan bring the butter to a white froth and stir in the flour. Be careful not to brown the mixture.

3. Stir in the cream and mix thoroughly. Add the shad roe.

4. Simmer for 5 minutes or until thick, stirring constantly, and slowly adding the salt, pepper, and lemon juice. Remove from the stove and set aside.

5. Separate the yolks of 3 eggs from the whites. Blend 2 of the yolks into the roe mixture. The third yolk may be discarded or preserved for a hollandaise sauce or any other use you wish.

6. Beat the egg whites until they form peaks, adding, about halfway through the beating process, a pinch of salt.

7. Fold the whites into the roe mixture.

8. Grease a 3-cup mold with butter, place it in a large pan half filled with hot water, and pour the roe mixture into the mold.

9. Steam the mixture in a 350°F oven for 30 minutes. Unmold in the usual manner and serve with Hollandaise or mayonnaise, and garnish with lemon wedges.

NOTE: the center of this mold may be filled with crabmeat, sweetbreads, spinach, or any number of foods. In this menu a filling is not necessary.

ST. GERMAIN SOUP

Soup of the evening, beautiful soup. When royalty arrives a soup must shortly follow. This saintly soup, as subtle as a sapphire seen by moonlight, is the favorite of Mr. Gardner Cowles, Chairman of the Board of Cowles Communications, Inc.

When Henri Soule was alive and presided over Le Pavillon, then New York's greatest restaurant, Mr. Cowles himself was able to live like royalty. He and his wife would drop in for dinner, ponder industriously over the menu, and at last place their order. The great Soule would then smile broadly at them and show them his book — he had written down the order the moment he saw them enter.

The first course, of course, was St. Germain Soup. The rest of the menu I have sworn to keep secret.

What You Will Need

2 pkgs. fresh frozen peas
1 cup boiling milk
1 cup beef broth
1 sprig mint
2 egg yolks
2 tbsps. butter
2 tbsps. flour
½ cup dry white wine
½ tsp. chervil
salt and pepper to taste

1. Normally I deplore the use of frozen vegetables, but in this country, for most of us, edible fresh peas are impossible to find even when in season. If you can find them, treat them like caviar. For St. Germain Soup, use frozen peas. Follow the instructions on the package, but reduce the cooking time by 3 minutes. Then set the peas aside.

2. Melt the butter in a heavy saucepan. When it is foaming, add the flour all at once and stir rapidly with a fork until it is quite thick.

3. Add the boiling milk — all at once — and cook over a low flame for about 3 minutes — until you have a nicely thickened sauce.

4. Add the remaining ingredients, one at a time, in any order — but save the wine until last. Simmer gently for a few minutes. If the soup appears too thin, add more wine.

5. Serve hot or cold, garnished with frosted mint leaves.

CROWN ROAST OF LAMB PETITE

When one thinks of a king one thinks of a crown, and in designing a menu, one thinks of a crown roast of lamb. This noble variation on the crown roast of lamb comes from Robert S. Bell, Chairman of the Board of Packard Bell. He last served it at a Commanderie de Bordeaux dinner to the delight of the members of that elite group. At that time it was served with both a '52 and '53 Chateau Margaux, for educational comparisons of these two great vintage years.

What You Will Need

A crown roast of lamb
   (made with 3 racks of lamb—
   about 18 chops)
3 pounds of ground leg of lamb
6 brandied peaches
¼ tsp. each: basil, chervil, cumin,
   rosemary, thyme, salt, and pepper
aluminum foil
6 minted pears

1. Have your butcher prepare the lamb racks in such a manner as to form a neatly proportioned, handsome crown.

2. Mix the herbs, salt, and pepper into the ground lamb. Stuff this mixture into the crown.

3. Cover the ends of the bones of lamb with aluminum foil to protect them.

4. Place the crown roast into a preheated 450°F oven. Immediately after putting the roast in the oven, reduce the heat to 350°F.

5. Let the roast hold court in the oven for 2 hours and 45 minutes.

6. A quarter of an hour before serving, heat the brandied peaches and minted pears in separate saucepans.

7. Remove the crown roast from the oven and place it on a silver serving platter. Discard the aluminum foil from the bones and garnish them with paper frills, if you like.

8. Surround the crown with hot whole brandied peaches and hot mint flavored pears; these are the jewels for the crown.

9. Pour a good glass of Bordeaux and enjoy life.

BRAISED EGG PLANT

This meal needs a vegetable, and since eggplant is one of the perfect complements to lamb, and since its skin is the rich dark purple of royalty, the choice is simple.

The skin of the eggplant, incidentally, is entirely edible. Yet it is usually discarded, even by the best of cooks, and even when served with the Greek dish "Moussaka." But no self-respecting Greek, king, or tycoon, should ever discard the tender, colorful skin of the eggplant in this recipe.

What You Will Need

3 large eggplants	1 cup tomato sauce
½ cup butter	½ cup finely chopped green pepper
½ cup finely chopped onions	2 cups beef broth
¼ cup lemon juice	1 cup dry white wine
1 tsp. basil	salt and pepper to taste

1. Slice the stems from the eggplant.
2. Cut the eggplant into bite-size cubes. Do not remove the skin.
3. Sprinkle the eggplant cubes with salt and lemon juice.
4. Let stand for 10 minutes. Drain off the juices.
5. While the eggplant is marinating, sauté the green pepper and onions in the butter.
6. Add the eggplant to the onions and green pepper. Then spoon in the rest of the ingredients, bring to a simmer, and continue to simmer, over a low flame, for 20 minutes.
7. Serve in wide, shallow soup bowls with all of the juices, either with the crown roast or as a third course. If you serve this dish as a third course you may continue pouring the wine throughout the course.

NOTE: You may serve a tossed green salad between this course and the dessert, if you like. *If* you like, then use either Henry Ford's French Dressing or Commander Whitehead's Lemon Dressing, which may be found in the Index. Should you be using an exceptional wine at this dinner, you should be sure that all of it has been drunk before presenting the salad.

CHOCOLATE SOUFFLE

Chocolate Souffle is the prince of desserts. It is truly meet, right, and salutary, then, that we have a Chocolate Souffle recipe from the Hon. Robert D. Murphy, Chairman of the Board of Corning Glass International. Mr. Murphy is by no means unpracticed in the art of entertaining kings, and this recipe was given him by an Italian named Gino, who was Mr. Murphy's personal chef when he was Ambassador to Brussels.

What You Will Need

2 tbsps. cold coffee
½ tsp. vanilla extract
3 eggs yolks, lightly beaten
4 egg whites, stiffly beaten
1 cup heavy cream, whipped

2 tbsps. butter
2 tbsps. flour
¾ cup milk
Pinch of salt
2 squares grated, unsweetened chocolate
⅓ cup sugar

1. Preheat oven to 350°F.

2. In a heavy saucepan, melt the butter until foaming.

3. Add the flour all at once and stir with a wire whisk until well mixed. Set aside.

4. In another saucepan, bring the milk to a boil. Add it, all at once, to the butter-flour mixture. Stir thoroughly with the whisk over a low flame until thick (about 30 seconds). Add the salt.

5. Set this mixture aside, and in a double boiler melt the chocolate with the sugar and coffee. When melted, add it to the egg sauce and blend it in.

6. Add the vanilla and blend.

7. Add the egg yolks, one at a time, blend, and cool.

8. Beat the egg whites until stiff, adding a pinch of salt once they start to foam.

9. When the egg whites are stiff, fold them into the chocolate mixture very gently with a rubber spatula. Do not try to mix them completely, for in doing so you will beat out the air bubbles that ultimately cause the souffle to rise.

10. Turn the souffle into a buttered, straight-sided, 2-quart casserole (or souffle dish or Charlotte Mold) sprinkled with sugar.

11. Bake 35 to 45 minutes at 350°F, or until puffed and brown. Serve immediately with whipped cream.

NOTE: A tablespoon of Grand Marnier folded into the whipped cream makes a regal touch for Chocolate Souffle.

Game People Eat

The Menu:

Shrimp Maison
Pheasant with Vermouth Sauce
or
Wild Duck Tamed
or
Steamed Quail on Toast
or
Poached Partridge
or
Venison Steak
Wild Rice
Pumpkin Chiffon Pie

The contributors: Mr. Malcolm Steiner, Universal Unlimited Inc.; Mr. Tex Cook, General Foods Corp.; Mr. Roy D. Chapin, Jr., American Motors Corp.; Mr. Marshall Field, of Field Enterprises Inc.; Mr. Robert D. Stuart, Jr., The Quaker Oats Co.; Mr. Bruno Pagliai, Tubos de Acero de Mexico, S.A.; Mr. Dean Witter, Dean Witter & Co.

SHRIMP MAISON

If horse racing is the sport of kings, hunting is the game of tycoons, as the distinguished list of contributors to this chapter indicates.

The distinctive flavor of game is not to everyone's taste, however, and those who like a wild duck may not like a pheasant. This menu gives four different kinds of game for the main course. My choices for the first course and the dessert remain the same. A shrimp dish makes an excellent opener, for shrimp may be purchased throughout the country, in markets in the most remote hunting regions, and is available at all times of the year. This recipe comes from Mr. Malcolm Steiner, President of Universal Unlimited, Inc., of Long Island.

What You Will Need

1 lb. of cooked shrimp	1 tbsp. Worcestershire sauce
4 hard boiled eggs, sieved	1 tbsp. fresh chopped parsley
2 tbsps. chili sauce	½ tbsp. salt
3 tbsps. mayonnaise	Freshly ground pepper to taste
1 tbsp. fresh lemon juice	1 pinch cayenne pepper

1. Press the hard boiled eggs through a medium sieve.

2. Chop the shrimps finely — fresh, frozen, or canned shrimp may be used.

3. Mix all of the ingredients in a lightly oiled, 3 cup bowl and refrigerate for 2 hours.

4. To serve, unmold the Shrimp Maison on a suitable plate or platter and garnish with radishes, scallions, cucumbers, and lemon wedges on a bed of lettuce. Or simply unmold the Maison on a lettuce bed and serve with thin, party rye bread.

PHEASANT OR PARTRIDGE WITH VERMOUTH SAUCE

This recipe comes from Mr. Marshall Field, who needs no further introduction. It is a recipe that Mr. Field invented himself, and uses on partridge and pheasant when he is shooting in New Hampshire or Illinois.

What You Will Need

2 pheasants	1 tbsp. currant jelly
2 apples	¼ tsp. garlic powder
½ cup dry vermouth	1 pinch curry powder
salt and pepper to taste	¼ cup heavy cream
1 tbsp. butter	1 tbsp. flour

1. Core and quarter the apples and stuff them into the cavity of the birds.

2. Salt and pepper the birds and roast them on a rack for 45 minutes at 450°F.

3. While roasting, baste every 15 minutes with the drippings and ¼ cup watered down vermouth (basting is important to prevent the birds from drying out).

4. Serve with a vermouth sauce made thusly:
   A. Melt 1 tablespoon of butter and 1 tablespoon of currant jelly in an iron skillet.
   B. Add the garlic powder, the curry powder, heavy cream, and ¼ cup dry vermouth.
   C. Stir in ½ cup of drippings and thicken with flour.
   D. Cook the sauce over slow heat until it is thick. Salt and pepper it to taste and serve it in a gravy boat.

WILD DUCK TAMED

This method of cooking wild duck was developed by Roy D. Chapin, Jr. (Chairman of the Board of American Motors Corp.), after many years of duck shooting. The instructions call for the duck to be cooked rather longer than some hunters prefer, yet in no way detracts from that certain, indefinable flavor. I suspect that Mr. Chapin would agree with me that the traditional method of serving duck, bloody and slightly rotten, requires courage rather than a healthy appetite on the part of those who must eat it.

What You Will Need

For One Duck:	
	salt and pepper
	⅔ cup honey
1 wild duck	⅓ cup orange juice
½ apple	⅓ cup cognac
½ cup chopped celery	2 oranges
1 bunch parsley	¼ cup grape jelly

1. Clean the duck thoroughly and pat dry with a paper towel.

2. Salt and pepper the cavity of the duck, then stuff it with celery, parsley, and ½ apple, sliced.

3. Roast the duck at 350°F, allowing 20 to 30 minutes per pound, and basting as often as possible with the following sauce:
   A. ⅔ cup honey
   B. ⅓ cup orange juice
   C. ⅓ cup cognac.

4. To serve, scoop cooked and seasoned wild rice in the center of a large platter. Spread grape jelly onto the edges of orange slices and arrange them around the rice. Place the breast of the duck on top of the rice and bring it to the table.

QUAIL ON TOAST

This is a southern method of preparing quail and comes from North Carolina tycoon Ben Cone of Cone Mills. Quail are abundant in North Carolina, and Mr. Cone hunts them with such a passion that he gives many of them away. One of the people he gives them to is his aunt, Mrs. Julius Cone, whose cook, Leola Parker, worked out this method of preparing them.

What You Will Need

1 quail for each serving (depending
   on the size of the bird)
2 tbsps. crisco
6 slices of toast, preferably made
   from homemade bread
6 thin slices baked Virginia ham
salt and pepper to taste
paprika to color
1 tbsp. butter

1. Split the quail along the back, salt and pepper the cavity, and dust the breast with paprika.

2. Melt the crisco in a large iron skillet together with the butter.

3. Brown the quail in the hot grease, then add 1 cup of water, cover the skillet, and steam for ½ to ¾ of an hour, or until tender.

4. Butter the toast, place 1 slice of warm Virginia ham on each slice of toast, and nestle a quail atop each slice of ham.

5. Top the quail with gravy made from the juices in the skillet and serve with wild rice and brandied peaches.

POULTRY STUFFING

If you would like to vary the stuffing for any of these birds, or just try a new kind of stuffing for a chicken or turkey, here is an unusual one from Robert D. Stuart Jr., President of the Quaker Oats Co. It was handed down to Mr. Stuart by his grandmother.

What You Will Need

2 cups old-fashioned oats
4 cups bread crumbs
½ cup melted butter
1 onion, grated
salt and pepper to taste
a little hot water

1. Pour just enough hot water over the oats to moisten them slightly (2 tbsps. should be enough). Let the oats stand and steam for 2 minutes.

2. Add the bread crumbs, butter, salt, pepper, and onions.

3. Pack the stuffing loosely into the bird of your choice, and roast the bird in the customary manner.

POACHED PARTRIDGE

Earlier in this book I presented several Mexican recipes contributed by American tycoons. Here is an "American" recipe from a Mexican tycoon.

Mr. Bruno Pagliai, the distinguished *presidente* of Tubos de Acero de Mexico, husband of Merle Oberon, and well deserved holder of the title "Mr. Mexico," enjoys hunting partridge, and here is his recipe for cooking them.

What You Will Need

6 partridges
1 stalk sliced celery
2 fistfulls whole pepper

¼ cup butter
2 cups white wine

1. Frankly, I do not understand the 2 fistfulls of pepper. If you are very brave, do with them what you will. If you are a coward, use 4 peppercorns. If you are undecided, wrap ½ cup of peppercorns in cheesecloth and add them to the broth.

2. But before you do all this, melt the butter in a large casserole for which you have a cover.

3. Add the wine and broth and celery and partridges.

4. Add the pepper in whatever quantity you dare.

5. Bring to a boil and simmer very, very gently for 2 hours.

6. Serve on toast or rice.

NOTE: If you think 2 fistfulls of pepper are unique, wait until you hear how Mr. Pagliai likes his chicken: "Take a deep pot. Put in 1 inch of rock-salt. Put one chicken, cleaned, over the salt. Cover with rock salt, about 1 inch thick. Place a cover over the pot and roast in a 400°F oven for 80 minutes. Break the salt and serve the chicken."

This dish has a sensational taste of its own.

VENISON STEAK

Mr. Dean Witter, General Partner of Dean Witter & Co., inherited this recipe from his parent's Chinese cook, who recently died, and who apprenticed, when a young man before the First World War, on a ranch in Nevada. The cook was taught this recipe by the Shoshone Indians. Naturally, some of the condiments have changed with the times and Mr. Witter has made the appropriate adjustments for them.

What You Will Need

¼ cup onion juice
1 cup heavy cream
1 tsp. sugar
¼ cup sherry
salt and pepper to taste
dash Maggi sauce (optional)

2 cups chicken broth
Haunch or rib of venison
1 cup flour
1 heavy paper bag
1 cup butter
dash Worcestershire sauce

1. Bone and strip the meat of fat and sinew.

2. Cut into ¼" steaks (cross-grain).

3. Pound each filet with the back of a knife.

4. Pour the flour into a paper bag and shake the steaks lightly around in it. Remove them from the bag and brush off excess flour.

5. Melt the butter in an iron frying pan, add the onion juice, and heat until it smokes.

6. Quick-fry (like hot cakes) both sides of the venison steaks in the butter and onion juice mixture. Place them on a serving platter.

7. Add the remaining ingredients to the juices in the pan, heat, stirring constantly, until you have a hot, runny, well mixed gravy.

8. Pour the gravy over the steaks and serve.

PUMPKIN CHIFFON PIE

Game is usually hunted in the autumn, when the pumpkins are ripe and orange. This different and delicate recipe for pumpkin pie comes from Tex Cook, Chairman of the Board of General Foods Corporation.

What You Will Need

1¼ tbsps. unflavored gelatin
¼ cup cold water
1 cup sugar
½ tsp. salt
½ tsp. ginger
½ tsp. nutmeg
½ tsp. cinnamon
1½ cups mashed canned pumpkin

⅔ cup milk
3 egg yolks
3 egg whites
1 baked, 8" pie shell, cooled
1 cup whipping cream
1 tsp. sugar
½ tsp. vanilla flavoring

1. Soak the gelatin in ¼ cup cold water.

2. Mix ½ cup sugar, the salt, and the spices in the top of a double boiler.

3. Add the pumpkin and milk, mix well, and place over boiling water until the mixture is hot.

4. Slowly stir the hot pumpkin mixture into the slightly beaten egg yolks. Return to the double boiler and cook 2 minutes, stirring constantly.

5. Remove from heat. Add the gelatin mixture and stir until the gelatin is completely dissolved. Cool the mixture until it begins to set.

6. Beat the egg whites until foamy throughout. Gradually add the remaining ½ cup of sugar, blending thoroughly with a spatula after each addition.

7. Fold the beaten egg whites into the pumpkin mixture and pour into the pie shell.

8. Chill in the refrigerator until firm. Serve with whipped cream flavored with 1 tsp. sugar and ½ tsp. vanilla flavoring.

A Barbequed Banquet
The Menu:
Callaway Special
Hickory Smoked Flank Steak
Chicken and Corn Diable
Romaine Salad Supreme
Glen Cove Cream

The contributors: Mr. Ely R. Callaway, Jr., Burlington Industries; Mr. Tex Cook, General Foods Corporation; Mr. Dan W. Lufkin, Donaldson, Lufkin & Jenrette, Inc.; Mr. Malcolm Steiner, Universal Unlimited Inc.; Mr. Robert Huyot, Inter-Continental Hotels.

CALLAWAY SPECIAL

The first image brought to the mind of a man cooking is that of a man barbequing. Most women avoid cooking out of doors. There is something in their intellectual attitude that prevents them from properly lighting the charcoals — not inability, I think, so much as vanity. The hair gets mussed, the mascara runs, the fingernails break or accumulate cinders.

Man's passion for barbequing probably lies deep in the brain, a vestigial remain from the days of the cave men, when all meals were cooked over an open flame.

Whatever the reason, no modern, respectable back yard is complete without a barbeque area, and no summer is complete without a banquet. In this chapter I offer the favorite barbeque recipes of three tycoons. Prepare them as three separate meals on various occasions throughout the summer, or spread them all out on a cedar table and invite a crowd.

The Callaway Special is a nourishing, delicious drink that replaces cocktails and the first course — serve it in paper cups while the embers glow. Mr. Callaway, the head of Burlington Industries, originated this drink, and where he lives it has become so popular that it is available as the "Callaway Special" at the refreshment stand on the golf courses at both the Wee Burn and Woodway Country Clubs. Minus the vodka or gin.

What You Will Need

18 ounces of tomato juice
10½ oz. beef broth (canned)
juice of 2½ juicy lemons
1 tsp. salt
1 tsp. freshly ground pepper
2 tsps. Worcestershire sauce
4 dashes Tabasco
½ tsp. thyme
1 tsp. celery salt
1 tsp. onion salt
a few sprigs of fresh dill
vodka or gin

Shake the ingredients vigorously together with 12 ice cubes. The vodka or gin should be added according to the host's discretion. One cup is not immoderate.

HICKORY SMOKED FLANK STEAK

This recipe comes from Tex Cook, Chairman of the Board of General Foods. Mr. Cook also provided the recipe for the Romaine Salad Supreme, which may be found below and is an excellent salad for a barbeque.

What You Will Need

1 flank steak (2 pounds)	½ cup cider vinegar
Seasoned meat tenderizer	3 tbsps. Worcestershire sauce
1 cup peanut oil	1 large onion, sliced.
¾ cup catsup	Hickory chips

1. Sprinkle the steak generously on both sides with the meat tenderizer; let it stand for at least 30 minutes.

2. In a shallow glass dish combine the salad oil, catsup, vinegar, and Worcestershire sauce; mix well.

3. Move the steak into the marinade. Spread the sliced onion over the steak, and if the marinade does not cover the steak, turn or baste it frequently. The steak should be permitted to marinate for 3 to 4 hours.

4. Soak a double handful of hickory chips in water while the charcoal fire is heating. When the fire is hot, toss the soaked hickory chips over it.

5. Place the steak on the grill about 3 inches above the fire. To keep the flame down, sprinkle the coals with water (use a sponge for this).

6. Cook about 8 minutes on each side, or until the desired degree of doneness is achieved.

7. To serve, slice the meat diagonally, across the grain, into very thin slices.

BACKYARD CHARCOAL GRILLED STEAK

Flank steak, of course, is not the only kind of steak — there are many others, and once you get involved in barbequing you will want to experiment with all of them. Here is a very special recipe for a Porterhouse steak grilled with cognac. It is an expensive but rewarding undertaking, and really tycoon fare.

The recipe comes from Mr. Robert Huyot, President of Inter-Continental Hotels, a huge hotel chain with facilities all over the world. Mr. Huyot, incidentally, is no novice at cook books — under his direction, and with the authoritative writing of Myra Waldo and the drawings of Rosalind Rust (who also illustrated *Tycoons In The Kitchen*), Mr. Huyot's firm published its own handsome cookbook, called "The Inter-Continental Gourmet Cookbook." His favorite recipe did not appear there. Here it is.

What You Will Need

6 lbs. steak—Porterhouse or New York
    cut (from strip loins.) The steaks
    should be roughly 2½ inches thick
1 garlic clove, cut in half
2 tbsps. melted butter
⅓ cup cognac (Three Star)
½ cup chopped parsley
salt and freshly ground black pepper
    to taste

1. Trim excess fat from the steak, and cut slits around the edges to prevent curling.

2. Rub all surfaces of the steak well with the garlic clove halves.

3. Use a portable "char-broil" unit, with hood. Keep the hood open, and grill the steak for 4 minutes over white hot charcoal (red hot briquettes covered with gray-white ash). Keep the steak as close to the heat as possible, so it will flame.

4. Turn the steak with a spatula and cook for another 4 minutes. This produces a good brown crust and seals in the juices.

5. Raise the grill to six inches above the coals and continue broiling to desired doneness (turning only once). During this phase you should keep the hood closed to insure a delicious, smoky flavor.

It is impossible for me to tell you how long to keep the steak for the "desired degree of doneness." Just as everyone's idea of "rare," "medium rare," "medium well," etc., varies, so varies each char-broil unit. The type of coals you use, the heat they are at, the time of day you cook the steak, the temperature — all affect the ultimate steak. Ten minutes of additional broiling would produce the kind of steak I like on the kind of equipment I have in a summer evening, under moonlight. But you must experiment. Suffice it to say that an undercooked steak is better than an overcooked one because it can be placed back in the broiler; and that a barbeque is always an adventure, and no one complains about an overcooked steak that has been cooked this way.

6. When the steak is done, remove it to a warm carving platter and cover with melted butter. Heat the cognac in a stainless steel ladle, over the charcoal heat, until warm enough to flame. Light it with a match and pour the flaming cognac over the buttered steak.

7. Garnish with finely chopped parsley, and season with salt and freshly ground pepper to taste.

8. Cut the steak on a 45 degree bias in ½ inch pieces and serve.

CHICKEN AND CORN DIABLE

This splendid recipe, which requires the presiding tycoon to marinate ears of corn in sea water for a half hour, comes from Dan W. Lufkin, of Donaldson, Lufkin & Jenrette, Inc., of the New York Stock Exchange. It was never cooked on Wall Street, but don't let that discourage you.

What You Will Need

For the Chicken:

2 broilers, quartered, with seasoning salt and freshly ground pepper rubbed in

For the Sauce:

½ cup catsup
1 cup vinegar
⅓ cup dark brown sugar
½ cup olive oil
2 tbsps. honey
1 tsp. cinnamon
1 tsp. dry mustard
3 dashes Tabasco
1 dash Worcestershire sauce
1 pinch tarragon

For the Corn:

1 unhusked ear per person (or 2 if desired) plus enough fresh sea water to cover the ears

1. Mix all sauce ingredients together and simmer the sauce over a low flame for 15 minutes, stirring constantly.

2. Marinate the chicken in the sauce for 2 hours.

3. Broil the chicken on an outdoor grill over low coals, basting frequently with the remaining sauce. The chicken will take roughly 40 minutes to cook.

4. Serve with fresh corn on the cob, cooked on the same grill in its husks. The corn should be soaked in sea water for a half hour before grilling. If you do not live near the sea, substitute lightly salted fresh water.

ROMAINE SALAD SUPREME
What You Will Need

1 large head romaine lettuce, washed,
    dried, and chilled
3 scallions, finely chopped
    (include green tops)
¾ tsp. finely chopped fresh mint
¼ tsp. oregano
salt and pepper to taste

1. Rub a chilled wooden salad bowl with a cut clove of garlic, if you like. This step may be omitted.

2. Add to the bowl the scallions, mint, oregano, toss together with the lettuce, and salt and pepper to taste.

3. For the dressing you will need:

1 egg
½ cup safflower oil
Juice of 1 lemon
¼ teaspoon salt

Combine these ingredients in a mixing bowl and beat with a rotary beater until foaming. Pour over the salad and toss.

4. To top the salad you will need:

½ cup grated Parmesan cheese
½ lb. bacon, cooked until crisp
2 or 3 tomatoes, peeled and cut
    into eighths
1 cup croutons

Sprinkle the salad with cheese; then crumble the bacon over the cheese. Arrange the tomatoes over the top and sprinkle with croutons.

GLEN COVE CREAM

This is an elaborate dessert that should be unmolded in the dead of summer under a full moon. The contributor is Mr. Malcolm Steiner, President of Universal Unlimited.

What You Will Need

1 envelope unflavored gelatin
2 tbsps. cold water
Three 1 oz. squares unsweetened chocolate
4 eggs, separated
dash of salt
A 9″ or 10″ springform

1 tbsp. vanilla flavoring
½ cup sugar
½ tsp. cream of tartar
¼ cup sugar
½ pint heavy cream
½ cup chopped walnuts
10 ladyfingers

1. Soften 1 envelope of gelatin in 2 tablespoons of cold water. Take three 1 ounce squares of unsweetened chocolate with ½ cup of water, place in a double boiler, and melt over low heat. Add the softened gelatin.

2. Separate the eggs. Beat the yolks together with ½ cup sugar, until a thread is formed. Add a dash of salt, a tablespoon of vanilla, blend thoroughly, and gradually add to the cooled chocolate and gelatin mixture.

3. Beat the egg whites until they are frothy. Add ½ teaspoon cream of tartar, then gradually add ¼ cup of sugar. Beat the egg whites until they are stiff. Gently fold this mixture into the chocolate mixture.

4. Beat the heavy cream until it forms peaks. Fold it into the chocolate and egg white mixture. The folding should be done with a rubber spatula, and should always be done gently.

5. Fold in the chopped walnuts.

6. Line the springform with the ladyfingers. Stand the ladyfingers vertically around the sides, lay them flat at the bottom. If you are using commercial ladyfingers (rather than homemade or French-bakery made), sprinkle a little cognac or cointreau over them to freshen them up and make them less repulsive.

7. Pour the chocolate cream over the ladyfingers and refrigerate overnight.

8. Remove the outer rim of the springform before serving.

A Dinner at Sea
The Menu:
Salad Nicoise
Seafood Supreme
Flaming Fruit

The contributors: Newton N. Minow, Leibman, Williams, Bennett, Baird & Minow; Lionel Billton, Billton Imports Ltd.

SALAD NICOISE

A dinner at sea, whether on a private yacht or a luxury liner, calls up a vision of the Mediterranean. Salad Nicoise is a French Riviera specialty, and very easy to do.

What You Will Need

3 boiling potatoes	2 tbsps. capers
1 cup cooked, French cut beans	4 tomatoes, quartered
12 fillets of anchovies	¼ cup olive oil
1 cup pitted ripe olives	1 tbsp. vinegar
salt and pepper to taste	1 tsp. chopped chervil
¼ cup chopped parsley	1 tsp. tarragon

1. Boil the potatoes in their skins. Cool them, peel the skins, and dice the potatoes.

2. Toss the potatoes together with the beans, the olives, the capers, olive oil, vinegar, salt, pepper, chervil, and tarragon.

3. Arrange the salad in individual salad bowls, decorate each salad with tomatoes and anchovies, and serve.

SEAFOOD SUPREME

This fragrantly flavored seafood dish is the favorite of Mr. Newton N. Minow, senior partner of Leibman, Williams, Bennett, Baird & Minow, a law firm. Mr. Minow, during the John F. Kennedy administration, was the U.S. Federal Communications Commission Chairman. He is also the originator of the famous remark: "Television is a vast wasteland." This recipe, he says, is for a "vast waistline."

What You Will Need

½ cup butter	6½ ounce can lobster
½ cup flour	1 large can crabmeat
3½ cups milk	½ lb. mushrooms
1 tsp. salt	½ lb. grated sharp cheddar
¼ tsp. pepper	¼ cup chopped green pepper
2 tsps. Worcestershire sauce	¼ cup pimiento
½ tsp. dry mustard	½ cup dry white wine
1 lb. shrimp	

1. Heat the butter in a heavy iron skillet until it is foaming.

2. Blend in the flour and stir until thick. Do not brown the flour.

3. In a separate saucepan, bring the milk to a boil and add it all at once to the flour and butter. Cook, stirring constantly, until the sauce is thick and smooth.

4. Add the seasonings, fold in the fish, mushrooms, and grated cheese, and continue cooking until the cheese is melted.

5. Stir in the green pepper, pimiento, and wine and simmer for 10 minutes. Serve in bowls or over rice.

FLAMING FRUIT

For a dinner at sea the dessert should be stunning and memorable, and certainly flaming. Not all tycoons are so enterprising as the tycoon in the drawing for this chapter, who managed to be lost at sea with a silver chafing dish. But Mr. Billton, of Billton Imports, may be, and this is his favorite dessert.

What You Will Need

2 cups fresh black cherries
1 cup pears, peeled and diced
1 cup red wine
1 quart vanilla ice cream

2 tbsps lemon juice
¼ cup sugar
½ cup cognac
1 chafing dish

1. Heat the wine and sugar in a chafing dish until the liquid is gently boiling.

2. Add the lemon juice and the fruit. Canned cherries and pears are perfectly acceptable, but be sure to use pitted cherries. Bring the liquid to just below the simmer stage and heat for 5 minutes.

3. Warm the cognac in a separate pan. Just before serving, pour the warm cognac over the fruit and ignite it with a match.

4. To serve, spoon the flaming fruit onto plates of vanilla ice cream.

Dinner at a Manhattan Penthouse
The Menu:
Bisque of Peas and Corn
Lamb Chops à ma Façon, with Port Sauce
Endive and Golden Delicious Salad
Ekmek Kadaif

The contributors: Henry J. Heinz II, H. J. Heinz Co.; Ezra K. Zilkha, American International Bank; Preston Frazier, Faroy Company.

BISQUE OF PEAS AND CORN

For many tycoons the whole purpose of success is a penthouse in Manhattan, resplendent with thick Persian carpets, spectacular views, and French maids in silk pajamas. Yet even a Manhattan penthouse presents difficulties. One of these was recently depicted in a cartoon in The New Yorker. The cartoon depicted a lady setting out the first course of a dinner on the penthouse terrace. The lady called her gentleman to table with these words: "Hurry up darling, your soup is getting dirty." (The cartoon was by R. B. Wilson.)

The black ash of pollution is the secret curse of penthouse living in Manhattan. One way to reduce its danger is to serve this bisque in covered, earthenware soupbowls, which will keep the bisque clean as well as warm. The recipe is the invention of Mr. Henry J. Heinz II, Chairman of the Board of the H. J. Heinz Company.

What You Will Need

1 package frozen peas in butter sauce	¾ cup light cream
1 package frozen corn in butter sauce	1 tsp. onion salt
¾ cup milk	

1. Heat the vegetables to serving temperature, according to the instructions on the package.

2. Puree the corn in a blender, and pass it through a coarse sieve to eliminate the hulls.

3. Add the peas and preheated milk and cream to the pureed corn. Blend quickly to a smooth consistency.

4. Reheat briefly, if necessary. Season to taste with onion salt and serve in warm, covered, earthenware bowls.

NOTE: For extra tang, ¼ cup dry sherry may be blended in at step 3.

LAMB CHOPS A MA FACON WITH PORT SAUCE

These lamb chops, which are the favorite of Mr. Ezra K. Zilkha, Chairman and Chief Executive Officer of the American International Bank, are protected from pollution by an exquisite crust. If you can avoid getting dirt on the crust it should be eaten, for it is very good indeed.

What You Will Need

6 double lamb chops	½ lb. melted butter
1 lb. filla dough*	¼ cup port
¼ lb. pate de foie gras	¼ lb. mushrooms

*Filla dough may be bought at any Greek or Middle Eastern store; if you cannot find it, use the pastry recipe for *Pirojkis*, which is given in detail in the chapter "*A Russian Dinner.*"

1. Spread a thin slice of foie gras on each lamb chop.

2. Wrap each chop separately in 5 layers of filla dough that has been cut in squares. Be sure the chops are tightly wrapped in the dough. If you are using the pastry recipe for Pirojkis, roll it out to $\frac{1}{8}$ of an inch, cut into 6 pieces, and wrap them around the 6 lamb chops.

4. Place the chops on a buttered, glass, ovenware dish and bake them in a 400°F oven until the dough is golden brown (30-40 minutes).

5. For the sauce, slice the mushrooms lengthwise and brown them in butter. Add the remaining foie gras and stir until smooth. Add the port, bring to a boil, stirring constantly, and serve in a gravy boat with the chops.

ENDIVE & GOLDEN DELICIOUS SALAD

This recipe is also from Mr. Zilkha, and the only way to keep it clean is to serve it under clear glass bells or vegetable bowls.

What You Will Need

1 lb. endives, washed and dried	1 lemon, juiced
2 golden delicious apples	6 glass bells
½ cup salad oil	3 tsps. wine vinegar

1. Slice the endives in the round.

2. Peel and slice the apples lengthwise and sprinkle with lemon juice.

3. Toss the apples and endives together with a dressing made of ½ cup salad oil and 3 teaspoons wine vinegar. Salt and pepper to taste, place on saucers, cover with glass bells, and serve.

EKMEK KADAIF

This dessert is an Armenian one, and a penthouse is the ideal place to prepare it, for the first step involves pouring cream into milk from a great height, and this causes such splattering that the only safe way to do it is in the nude; carryings-on such as this are commonplace in penthouses.

The recipe is the favorite of Mr. Preston Frazier, President of Faroy Inc., who invented a remarkable series of candles in the form of tomatoes, eggplants, and now, even eggs. The candles make delightful decorations for an evening in the penthouse garden.

What You Will Need

8 slices of zwieback	1 quart of milk
2 cups hot water	1 pint heavy cream
juice of 2 lemons	a good deal of time and patience
2 cups honey	

1. Arrange 8 slices of zwieback (or Holland Rusks) in a shallow pan.

2. Add 2 cups of hot water mixed together with the juice of 2 lemons. When the zwieback are puffed and soft, pour off the excess water and pour over the zwieback 2 cups of honey.

3. Bake in a 350°F oven for 45 minutes. Cool to room temperature, cover, and set aside.

4. To make the "kaymak," or sauce, for these little cakes, place 1 quart of milk in a large, shallow enamel saucepan.

5. Bring the milk to a *very slow simmer*. If there is any question in your mind as to whether the simmer is low enough, asssume that it is.

6. From as high as possible — stand on a chair if you are short or have short arms — pour 1 pint of cold, heavy cream into the milk. This is a preposterously messy process but an essential one.

7. Continue to simmer, uncovered, for 2 hours. *Once the cream is in the pan never touch the pan or move it in any way.*

8. Turn off the heat or flame and let the kaymak stand in its pan, without touching it, for 7 hours.

9. Bring back to a low simmer for 30 minutes. Turn off the flame and cool the kaymak to room temperature.

10. Transfer the pan to the refrigerator. Let it sit for 24 hours.

11. At the end of 24 hours you will find, floating on top, a thick, delicious stuff that somewhat resembles marshmallows. Remove this, cut into small squares, and place one square on top of each Zwieback.

12. Serve in small portions with dry champagne or black coffee.

Soup for Lunch

The Menu:

Oxtail Stew
Tossed Green Salad
French Bread
Date and Nut Dessert

The contributor: Mr. Bernard F. Gimbel, Gimbel Brothers, Inc.

OXTAIL STEW

The late Bernard Gimbel, the man behind a store so famous that it is known to people who have never been within a thousand miles of it, and an ardent worker for the improvement of New York City, died at age 81, on Sept. 29, 1966. His passing left a considerable gap in the dwindling group of New York City's grand old men.

Mr. Gimbel's favorite recipe was Oxtail Stew. It is a wonderful conversation piece and a perfect stew for lunch.

What You Will Need

1 tsp. cooking oil	2 fresh carrots, sliced
1 oxtail per serving	1 box frozen peas
1 cup baby onions	salt, pepper to taste
1 clove garlic, chopped	water
1 bay leaf	

1. Clean the oxtails carefully, removing any tiny bone slivers with a small, sharp knife.

2. Place the tails in a saucepan with a small amount of cooking oil.

3. Add the garlic and onions and enough salt (about a teaspoon) to prevent the tails from sticking.

4. Cook over a moderate flame for 15 minutes, or until the tails are evenly browned.

5. Add 2 cups cold water for each oxtail. Add the bay leaf, bring to a boil and simmer slowly for two hours.

6. Add the carrots and simmer for another 10 minutes.

7. Add the frozen peas, simmer another 10 minutes, and serve.

BREAD FOR THE STEW

When you are having a soup or stew for lunch, a simple tossed green salad and French bread add just the right touch.

To make a delicious and unusual bread, buy an uncut loaf of French or Italian bread and slice not quite to the bottom crust — so that the loaf still holds together at the bottom. Spread generous clumps of butter and tiny slivers of garlic between the slices, and then alternately insert slices of peeled cucumber and Swiss cheese between the slices of bread. Heat in a 400F oven until the cheese is soft, the bread warm and crisp, but tender inside, and the butter melted. This makes a spectacular bread for any meal.

DATE AND NUT DESSERT

Here is a warm, chewy, luscious desert that will tempt the most devoted calorie counter to forsake his diet. It is "different" and surprisingly simple to do.

What You Will Need

1½ cups brown sugar	1 tsp. baking powder
2 cups water	½ cup dates
1 tbsp. butter	½ cup chopped walnuts
½ cup milk	1½ cups heavy cream
1 cup sifted flour	

1. Boil together the 2 cups of water and 1 cup of brown sugar and pour them into a bread pan or a casserole.

2. Mix 1 tbsp. butter, ½ cup brown sugar, ½ cup milk, 1 cup flour, 1 tsp. baking powder, ½ cup chopped dates, and ½ cup chopped walnuts. This makes a nice dough.

3. Drop the dough into the liquid in the bread pan. Do not stir it.

4. Bake for 30 minutes at 375F, remove from the oven, spoon onto dessert plates, and serve with sweet cream.

Oysters for Lunch

The Menu:

Oyster Stew
Oyster Crackers
French Bread
Cole Slaw
Apricot Surprise

The contributor: Mr. James A. Drain, Joy Manufacturing Co.

OYSTER STEW

Oyster Stew is surrounded by an enormous mystique, but I think we can crash through it here simply by saying that Mr. Drain, President and Chief Executive Officer of Joy Manufacturing, has provided us with the recipe used at the Oyster Bar of Grand Central Station. Many gourmets and most commuters will assure you that this particular oyster bar has perfected and immortalized the art of cooking oysters.

What You Will Need (for 2 servings)

1 pint fresh oysters	1 teaspoon Worcestershire Sauce
1 cup cream	pinch of celery salt
2 cups milk	pinch of paprika
2 tbsps. butter	salt and pepper to taste

1. The trick is to put the oysters with their juice into a *double boiler*. Add to a pint of oysters butter the size of two walnuts, the Worcestershire Sauce, and the seasonings.

2. Heat the oysters in a double boiler until their skirts begin to curl.

3. Add the milk and cream mixture and continue heating until eating temperature is reached (165F). Do not boil the stew.

This process, in Mr. Drain's words, "keeps the oysters tender and juicy rather than, as we so often find them, having the consistency of an old tennis shoe sole."

COLE SLAW

Cole slaw, like most salads, varies with practically every cook. I do not disapprove of cole slaw that is touched up with chili powder, mayonnaise, pineapple chunks, or what have you. But for a fairly rich dish such as oyster stew the slaw is better in a purer form, such as the one below.

What You Will Need

1 quarter of a cabbage, shredded	¼ cup tarragon vinegar
1 carrot, shredded	2 tbsps. sugar

1. Dissolve the sugar in the vinegar, and toss the dressing together with the cabbage and the carrots.

APRICOT SURPRISE

This dish, with its graham cracker crust and pungent apricots, provides a tasty but practical dessert that will not detract from the taste of oyster stew, still lingering on the palate.

What You Will Need

½ cup melted butter
1 large can apricots, pitted
10 graham crackers
½ cup sugar

1 pint heavy cream
2 tsps. sugar
1 tsp. vanilla extract

1. Crush with a rolling pin or whisky bottle enough graham crackers to make a crust that will hold enough servings for the number of people you are inviting for lunch. Ten graham crackers should be sufficient for 6 guests.

2. Add the melted butter and a half cup of sugar to the crushed crackers.

3. Line half of the crushed crackers in the bottom of a 9 inch pie plate.

4. Drain the apricots and arrange them on top of the graham cracker crust. Cover the apricots with the remaining crackers.

5. Heat in a 300F oven for 20 minutes. Serve warm with cold, sweetened whipped cream.

An Old-Fashioned Lunch

The Menu:

Jellied Eggs
Collops
Pears Pumpkin

The contributor: Mr. John Walker, The National Gallery of Art.

JELLIED EGGS

If you carefully save your beef bones and boil them down for consomme or broth you may use your own stock for the jellied eggs. If you do not you may substitute any prepared beef consomme with gelatin added.

What You Will Need

6 leaves of lettuce	6 lemon wedges
6 cups beef consomme, jellied	6 sprigs of parsley
6 tsps. sherry	1 truffle (optional)
6 hard boiled eggs	dash of Worcestershire Sauce

1. Hard boil the eggs, cool them, peel, and slice.

2. Slice the truffle into six slices; press the slices into the yolk of the six largest egg slices.

3. Pour the consomme into a mixing bowl, add the sherry and the Worcestershire Sauce, mix, and set aside.

4. Arrange the egg slices in six consomme cups or individual mousse molds. Be sure that each serving gets one of the truffle-stuffed egg slices.

5. Pour the consomme over the eggs, and refrigerate for three hours or until set. To serve, unmold on a bed of lettuce and garnish with sprigs of parsley and lemon wedges.

COLLOPS

It is not easy to know what to say about Collops. It is not even easy to know what they are. One runs across the word from time to time in English literature, and if one consults the Oxford Dictionary one finds that the origin of the word is obscure — that it can mean, or has meant, so remote a dish as a fried egg served atop bacon, and that the word is now used principally in Scotland and means, more or less, meat cut into small pieces.

Collops is the favorite of Mr. John Walker, the Director of the National Gallery of Art in Washington, D.C., and former Director of the American Academy in Rome. This recipe he cooks himself. It is dazzlingly simple.

Mr. Walker says: "Collops are very simple to do and were among the favorite Scotch dishes in the 18th century. Samuel Johnson was given them constantly when he did his tour of the Hebrides, though how much he enjoyed them I do not know. In any case, they were usually of lamb, lamb being cheaper than beef. Lamb collops are ghastly. Oddly enough, the recipe is hard to come by. I remember my grandfather saying he had to get it out of Chamber's *Information For The People,* an old Scotch encyclopedia."

140

Collops are so simple that many people find them dull, and are tempted to add spices, a bit of tomato sauce, onions, sour cream, and mushrooms. This is fine, but it is not collops. It is Hamburger Stroganoff.

If you are a purist, fond of the past, I think you will want to follow Mr. Walker's recipe closely.

What You Will Need

3 pounds ground beef (neck, round, or tenderloin)	1 cup fresh parsley salt and pepper to taste
2 tbsps. butter	1 cup cold water

1. Cover the bottom of an iron skillet with cold water.
2. Place the skillet over a medium flame and add the ground beef.
3. Break up the beef and stir it constantly. When it is slightly gray on the outside, but while there is still a touch of pink (the meat will now be rather dry), season heavily, remove to a serving dish, and dot with small pieces of butter and parsley.
4. Serve over noodles, toast, rice, or mashed potatoes.

PEARS PUMPKIN

I found this extraordinary recipe on the subway one night, written in purple ball point pencil on the margins of the pages of The New Republic. Why it is called "pumpkin" is a mystery to me.

What You Will Need

3 pears (or six canned half pears)	6 tbsps. Cointreau
6 generous scoops peppermint ice cream	2 squares sweetened chocolate

1. Place the 6 pear halves in dessert bowls.
2. Melt the chocolate squares.
3. Scoop the mint ice cream into the pear hollows, pour a tablespoon of cointreau over each, and drip the melted chocolate over the whole works. Serve with confidence.

An Italian Lunch

The Menu:

Stracciatella
Harry's Shrimps
Tossed Green Salad
Sop in the Pan

The contributors: Mr. Enrico Mariotti, Harry's Bar; Mr. Hendrik Cleton, FA F. J. Cleton.

STRACCIATELLA

Stracciatella is a hot variation of the jellied eggs in Chapter XV. The ingredients are roughly the same, but the method of preparation is so different that you normally wouldn't associate the two soups at all. Stracciatella is standard Italian fare and is served throughout the country.

What You Will Need

6 cups beef broth or consomme
3 eggs
1 tbsp. sherry

1 tsp. Worcestershire sauce
6 tsps. grated parmesan cheese

1. Pour the consomme, the sherry, and the Worcestershire Sauce into a saucepan and bring it to a boil.

2. While it is heating, break three eggs into a small bowl and whip them thoroughly with a fork.

3. When the broth boils remove it from the heat, quickly pour in the beaten eggs, and stir rapidly for 20 seconds. Serve with grated parmesan cheese.

HARRY'S SHRIMP

This is the second choice of Enrico Mariotti, who is described more fully in Chapter X. The dish is easy to prepare and presents only one problem: fish broth. Fish broth is made by boiling down the heads, tails, and bones of fish. The next best thing is to use clam juice, which tends to be overly salty. A last resort is to boil up the shells of the shrimp, and if all fails you may subsitute chicken broth.

What You Will Need

36 fresh shrimps, peeled and cleaned
6 tbsps. butter
1 cup French cognac
½ cup fish broth
½ cup dry white wine

½ cup heavy cream
3 egg yolks, well beaten
1 scallion, chopped
juice of ½ lemon
salt and pepper to taste

1. Melt the butter until it is foaming. Add the flour all at once and stir rapidly until it makes a fine paste. Then pour in the cognac and the stock, and when you have carefully blended it, add the cream in driblets and then the egg yolks, one at a time.

2. Add the lemon juice, salt and pepper, and cook until the sauce is moderately thick. Set it aside.

3. Peel and clean the shrimp.

4. Chop the scallion finely.

5. Sauté the scallion for 2 minutes in butter in a heavy skillet. Add the shrimp. Turn the heat up for 1 minute, or until the shrimp are nicely browned. Reduce the heat and simmer the shrimp for 5 minutes, or until they are tender. Overcooking will make them tough and dry.

6. Serve the shrimp on toast or Rice Pilaff, with the sauce poured over them. Enrico's recipe for Rice Pilaff may be found in Chapter X. Substitute fish broth for chicken broth in making the rice for this dish.

SOP IN THE PAN

Tycoons seem especially fond of French toast, in one form or another. And they all seem to agree (or at least the 14 tycoons who sent me recipes for French Toast) that it is a great thing to serve late at night, especially after a busy evening. The basic recipe for French Toast appears in the *Miscellaneous* section of this book. The recipe below is from Hendrik Cleton, Managing Director of F. J. Cleton — a Dutch company. Mr. Cleton's recipe may be used as a dessert, and a most unusual one it makes. If one substitutes an orange-flavored liqueur for the brandy one could call it "Mock Crepes Suzette." Here is Mr. Cleton's description of his favorite dish:

"It concerns here just a simple, but favorite recipe, either for an entree, dessert, or whole meal, for those events when you have to take care of yourself in a bachelor-like way. So, when you have lots of stale bread, you are tired (or perhaps lazy) and have a roaring appetite!"

What You Will Need

6 slices of stale bread	6 tsps. brandy
3 eggs	sugar and cinnamon
1⅓ cups milk	(to sprinkle over each serving)
6 tbsps. butter	

1. Whip the eggs, add the milk, and then the brandy.

2. Dip one by one into this mixture the slices of crustless, stale bread. Let each slice of bread completely absorb the liquid.

3. Place a dollop of butter in the frying pan and heat it until it foams.

4. Sauté the slices of bread one by one (or two together if you have a large enough pan) on both sides equally until they become a nice yellowish brown. Keep them warm on a heated plate, sprinkle them with sugar and cinnamon — and *bon appetit!*

A British Luncheon

The Menu:

Scotch Smoked Soup
Steak and Kidney Stew
Tossed Green Salad
Fruit Cocktail Romanoff

The contributors: Mr. Lionel Billton, Billton Imports Ltd.; Mr. George J. Hecht, Parents Magazine Enterprises, Inc.

SCOTCH SMOKED SOUP

Mr. Lionel Billton's Scotch Smoked Soup is one of the most fragrant and certainly the most unique soups that I have ever eaten. If you have your own favorite recipe for mushroom soup, by all means use it here. But this recipe will transport the most dreary canned cream of mushroom soup into a Scottish heaven.

What You Will Need

1 cup button mushrooms	4 cups mushroom soup
1 cup mince kippered herring	½ cup Scotch whiskey

1. Mince the kipper thoroughly with a fork or a blender. Be careful to remove all pieces of bone and gristle.

2. Combine the kipper and the soup and mushrooms together in a sauce pan and heat slowly to 180F.

3. Just before serving add the Scotch whisky. Serve to a sober gathering.

STEAK & KIDNEY STEW

If you have never thought of eating a kidney, or if you have been afraid to, or if you have tried kidneys and not liked them, I strongly advise you to forget all past experience or fears and try this recipe. It puts kidneys into such an attractive light that it may reform you entirely. And if you simply cannot face kidneys, substitute chicken livers.

This recipe, also the favorite of Mr. Billton, is a traditional English dish, often served in pie or pudding form.

What You Will Need

2 pounds round steak	1 tsp. paprika
4 lamb or veal kidneys	½ tsp. basil
1 large yellow onion	1 cup beef stock
1 cup red wine	1 pound button mushrooms

1. Chop the onion and sauté it in butter until it is golden. Remove the onion from the pan.

2. Chop the steak into bite-size pieces, brown it quickly in the pan, remove, and set aside.

3. In the same pan sauté the kidney for 5 minutes, after removing fat and filament.

4. Slice kidneys diagonally and return to pan with steak and the remaining ingredients.

5. Simmer gently for 30 minutes. Serve in bowls over potatoes, noodles, or rice.

NOTE: This dish may be made ahead of time and will keep in the refrigerator for 10 days.

FRUIT COCKTAIL ROMANOFF

Mr. George F. Hecht, Chairman of the Board of Parents Magazine Enterprises Inc., appears to be fond of desserts; this simple, pretty dessert makes a colorful topping to the hearty courses that precede it. It has a Russian-sounding name, but a distinctly British flavor.

What You Will Need

1 can of fruit cocktail	1½ cups milk (according to
½ cup Cointreau	instructions on pudding mix)
1 package vanilla	1 pint vanilla ice cream
flavored pudding mix	minted cherries

1. Drain the fruit, place it in a bowl, pour the Cointreau over it, and chill.

2. Prepare the pudding, following the directions on the package but reducing the milk by one-half cup. Cool the pudding and stir the fruit mixture into it. Chill again.

3. Cut the ice cream, which should be solidly frozen, into small cubes and fold into the pudding just before serving.

4. Garnish with the minced cherries and serve at once in champagne or sherbet glasses.

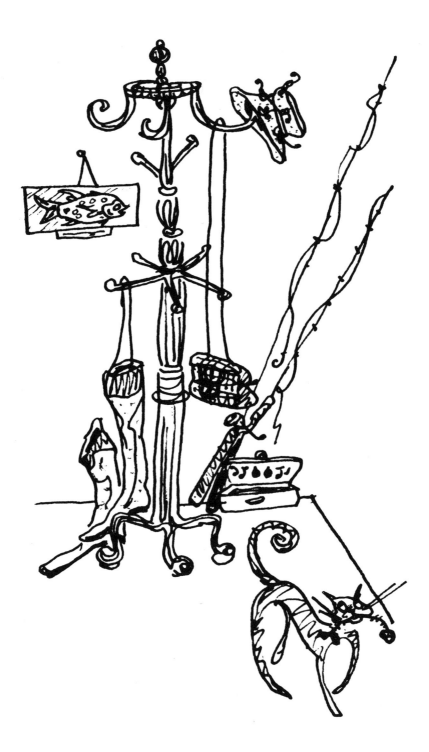

Fish for Lunch

The Menu:

Zuppa di Fagioli alla Toscana
Dover Sole
Young Boiled Potatoes
Tossed Green Salad
Apples and Nuts

The contributors: Mr. Elliott Haynes, Business International; Mr. G. H. Beeby, British Titan Products Co. Ltd.

ZUPPA DI FAGIOLI ALLA TOSCANA

Mr. Elliott Haynes, the publisher of *Business International,* first sampled this dish in Rome, though its true home is north of Rome, in Tuscany.

In Tuscany the beans are large and white (see Chapter III). In America, Great Northern beans are the closest things to them. You may use ordinary tap water for this recipe, but I do believe a distilled water makes a tastier soup.

What You Will Need

1 pound Great Northern Beans	1 ham bone (with plenty of meat)
1 stalk celery, with leaves	2 bay leaves
1 carrot	salt and pepper to taste
1 large tomato	4 quarts of water

1. Soak the beans overnight in enough tap water to cover them.
2. Pour out this water and add the four quarts of fresh water.
3. Chop up the carrot, celery, and the tomato and add them, together with the ham bone and the seasonings, to the water.
4. Bring to a boil and simmer gently until the beans are soft to the touch — about three hours.
5. Serve the soup in large, deep bowls with a sprinkling of grated parmesan cheese on top.

NOTE: The longer this soup sits the better it gets.

DOVER SOLE

Mr. Beeby has already given us his recipe for roast beef. His second choice is equally British. Mr. Beeby writes that Dover Sole can only be bought in areas around the North Sea, and *technically,* of course, he is correct. But the so-called "English Sole" that is available in most fish markets is, I think, very good. Flounder is less expensive and not quite in the same class, but even flounder has its fans and makes an acceptable substitute. Do not try to pass it off as sole, though. Announce it as flounder and your guests will be happy and well fed.

What You Will Need

6 fillets of Dover Sole	¼ cup flour
(12 if the fillets are small)	½ cup butter
(or "English" sole or flounder)	1 paper bag

1. Place the flour in the paper bag.

2. Slip the fillets of sole into the paper bag, toss them gently, and remove them to a platter. Shake off any excess flour. Each fillet should be lightly coated.

3. Heat 1/3 of the butter in a heavy iron skillet until foaming. Carefully lay two of the fillets into the pan and sauté quickly, 3 minutes on one side, 2 on the other. Do not burn or overly brown the fillets. They should be golden in color, with just a hint of brown.

4. Repeat the cooking process, adding more butter for the additional fillets.

5. Serve immediately with lemon wedges and parsley.

THE VEGETABLES

Serve a tossed green salad for the green vegetables. Mr. Beeby recommends the small, young potatoes some call French, some call Irish, and some call Russian. Boil them in their skins and serve them with plenty of melted butter.

If you serve wine with the lunch, Mr. Beeby's favorite with this meal is a cold Mersault or Chablis. And he urges the elimination of "Tartar Sauce," which he feels ruins the fish. I am in complete accord with him on this matter.

THE DESSERT

Use a simple dessert for this meal — one that can be prepared with no effort, but that is refreshing and healthy. To wit: apples and nuts. Select juicy red apples and serve them on saucer with a fruit knife. Serve the nuts — preferably walnuts — in their shells with nutcrackers.

A Fourth of July Lunch
The Menu:
Salmon Mousse
White Asparagus with Mayonnaise
Purloined Blueberries

The contributors: Mr. Malcolm Steiner, Universal Unlimited; Mr. John Elliott Jr., Ogilvy & Mather.

SALMON MOUSSE

This meal comes in three colors — red, white, and blue. How patriotic. How Fourth of July. The first dish, the red one, was forwarded to me by Malcolm Steiner, President of Universal Unlimited. It is a tasty and nourishing dish for a hot summer day.

What You Will Need

1 tbsp. unflavored gelatin	¼ cup mayonnaise
1 small onion	1 lb. canned salmon
2 tbsps. lemon juice	1 tsp. fresh dill
½ cup boiling water	¼ tsp. paprika
¼ cup sour cream	1 cup sweet cream

1. Blend the gelatin, the onion, the lemon juice, and the boiling water in a blender for 1 minute.

2. Add all of the remaining ingredients except the sweet cream and blend for 1 minute.

3. Add the cream a little at a time, blending for a few seconds each time the cream is added.

4. Pour the mixture into a fish mold and chill for three hours, or until set.

5. To serve, unmold the mousse and ladle a sauce over it if you like. A good sauce for the mousse may be made quite easily by shredding a small cucumber and blending it into a cup of sour cream, a small, finely grated onion, a sprig of dill, and a tablespoon of lemon juice.

WHITE ASPARAGUS

Fresh white asparagus is nearly impossible to find, but the canned variety, usually imported from Germany, though expensive is superb. Serve it chilled with mayonnaise or hollandaise sauce.

PURLOINED BAKED BLUEBERRIES

This is a great dessert when fresh blueberries are in season and is absurdly easy to do. The recipe comes from John Elliott Jr., Chairman of the Board of Ogilvy & Mather. It is called "Purloined" because Mrs. Elliott stole it from Mrs. Ogilvy, who stole it from Mrs. Whitehead, the Commander's wife.

Tycoons marry resourceful women. This is a good do-it-yourself dessert, for you may prepare it ahead of time and bake it while the main course is being served.

What You Will Need

3 boxes blueberries
Graham cracker crust
1 cup dark brown sugar
1 cup heavy cream

1. Wash the blueberries in a collander and spoon them into a souffle dish (1½ quart), alternating with heaping tablespoons of dark brown sugar.

2. Prepare a graham cracker crust according to the directions on the package, and press it down over the blueberries lightly.

3. Bake at 350°F for 25 minutes and serve immediately with heavy cream.

Lunching in Style
The Menu:
Salad Nouveau
Shad Roe Souffle
That Rum Thing

The contributors: Mr. Bill Blass, Bill Blass Inc.; Mr. John Elliott Jr., Ogilvy and Mather.

SALAD NOUVEAU

Unusual and surprising combinations are the lifeblood of the world of fashion, and they give food a lift, too. This salad is nothing if not chic. It is also full of vitamins.

What You Will Need

2 avocados	2 cups watercress
2 cups strawberries	¼ cup vegetable oil
salt and pepper to taste	1 lemon
½ cup chopped green pepper	

1. Peel and slice the avocados and sprinkle a little salt on them so they don't turn brown.

2. Wash the strawberries and slice them in half.

3. Mix the strawberries, avocados, watercress, and green pepper together with the vegetable oil and the juice from one lemon. Toss, season with salt and pepper, and serve chilled.

SHAD ROE SOUFFLE

Broil it, fry it, make a sauce of it, turn it into a mousse, create a souffle — shad roe is always a winner with tycoons. This recipe is from Bill Blass, famed New York designer of men's and women's fashions. Although New York is a restaurant lunch town, Mr. Blass likes having lunch at his home, and in the spring, when roe is in season, he frequently prepares this dish. The making of a souffle is one of the more pleasant challenges of life. If you follow these instructions carefully, you should have no trouble producing a fool-proof dish.

What You Will Need

2 pairs shad roe	¾ cup milk
½ tsp. salt	1 tbsp. chopped chives
1 tbsp. lemon juice	4 egg yolks, lightly beaten
6 tbsps. melted butter	6 egg whites, stiffly beaten
¼ cup all-purpose flour	1 tsp. salt
	½ tsp. white pepper

1. Preheat the oven to 375°F.

2. Place the shad roe in a shallow pan, cover with water, and simmer for 10 minutes.

3. Remove the roe from the water and cool. Reserve 2 tablespoons

of cooking water. Break the roe into small pieces and add salt, lemon juice, and 2 tablespoons of melted butter.

4. Blend flour into the remaining butter in the saucepan. Slowly add the reserved cooking liquid and the milk, stirring constantly. Bring to a boil while stirring and simmer for one minute. Add the salt, pepper, and chives.

5. Add the egg yolks and shad roe to the sauce.

6. Beat the egg whites until they form stiff peaks and carefully fold them into the shad roe sauce.

7. Pour the mixture into a 2 quart souffle dish. Bake for 30 minutes at 375°F. Then bake 5 minutes longer at 400°F. The souffle is done when it is nicely puffed and browned.

THAT RUM THING

That's what John Elliott of Ogilvy and Mather calls this childishly simple but delicious dessert.

What You Will Need

1 quart coffee ice cream
1 cup chocolate coffee beans
1 cup dark rum

1. If you are being fancy, get a melon mold of coffee ice cream; if not, simply scoop the ice cream into a pretty bowl.

2. Sprinkle with chocolate beans — the crunchy kind with liquid centers, not the milk chocolate ones.

3. Pour a liberal amount of dark rum over the ice cream and serve immediately.

Ten Tasty Suppers for Sunday Night
  The Selections:
  Onion Pie
  Joe's Special
  Cutlets Kiev
  Chile Con Carne
  Hobo Scramble
  Vegetable Soup
  Johnny Cakes and Dried Beef Gravy
  Scallopini—Quick and Easy
  Swiss Fondue
  Easy Stroganoff

ONION PIE

Sunday night is the time for a light, quick supper, and in this chapter I present ten recipes that tycoons like to eat for Sunday supper. Onion Pie comes from Newton N. Minow, Senior Partner of Leibman, Williams, Bennett, Baird & Minow and former FCC Chairman.

What You Will Need

2½ cups onions
½ lb. grated sharp cheddar cheese
30 soda crackers
½ cup melted butter
3 eggs
1½ cups milk
½ tsp. pepper
½ tsp. salt

1. Make a crust of melted butter and soda crackers rolled fine. Line a casserole with the crust, slice the onions thinly and sauté them in butter, and lay them in the casserole. Add the grated cheese.

2. Scald the milk, beat the eggs lightly, and mix them together. Add the salt and pepper.

3. Pour the egg and milk mixture over the onions and bake for 50 minutes at 350°F.

JOE'S SPECIAL

This recipe comes from Fairfax M. Cone, Director of Foote Cone & Belding, Inc. "Joe's" is an old San Francisco restaurant where the opera high silk hats and teamster's leather caps sit side by side at the long counter. The "Special" is special indeed.

What You Will Need

1 clove garlic, chopped
4 tbsps. olive oil
1 lb. ground beef
1 cup chopped, cooked spinach
4 eggs
½ tsp. pepper
1 tsp. salt

1. Sauté the garlic in olive oil until it is soft.

2. Add the ground beef, and cook for 2 minutes over a medium flame. When the meat is just about cooked, add the chopped spinach and heat again.

3. When the spinach is hot, add the eggs and scramble. Salt and pepper to taste and serve immediately. Do not overcook. The eggs should be light and tender.

CUTLET KIEV

The recipe for this famous Russian dish, of French origin, some say, comes from Col. Serge Obolensky. When you sit down to eat it, warn your guests to protect themselves with napkins, for as you cut into the cutlets the butter inside has a tendency to spurt out.

What You Will Need

1 deboned chicken breast for each person	¼ cup chopped parsley
½ pound butter	1 cup bread crumbs
	2 raw eggs, lightly beaten

1. Take a chicken breast that has been deboned, place it on a chopping board, and lay several pieces of waxed paper over it.

2. Flatten the chicken breast with a meat pounder or the back handle of a knife. This step should be done gently or you will pound the meat to pieces.

3. Sprinkle a little parsley on the meat and nestle a ball of cold butter about the size of a walnut on top of the parsley. Fold the chicken around the butter to form a ball.

4. Dip the ball into the beaten eggs and then into the bread crumbs. Repeat the performance for the remaining chicken breasts.

5. Sauté the cutlets in butter for 10 minutes and serve with a white sauce flavored with Marsala wine.

CHILI CON CARNE

This recipe is from Mr. William R. Salomon, Managing Partner of Salomon Brothers & Hutzler — the world's largest bond brokers. Mr. Salomon says about his recipe: "This is what we enjoy for early supper on a cold Sunday evening. The best place to eat it is our kitchen."

What You Will Need

4 cups canned red kidney beans	2½ cups canned tomatoes
2 lbs. ground beef	4 tbsps. chili powder
2 cups sliced onion	½ tsp. crushed red pepper
3 garlic cloves, minced	¾ tsp. oregano
¼ cup olive oil	1 tsp. salt

1. Sauté the onion, garlic, and beef in oil for 10 minutes.

2. Add the other ingredients, cover, and simmer for 30 minutes. Serve hot.

TOM PACK'S HOBO SCRAMBLE

This Southern style recipe comes from Mr. Barry Bingham, editor and publisher of The Courrier-Journal and The Louisville Times. Mr. Bingham, who is known in some circles as "Mr. Kentucky," got this recipe from his grandfather. Tom Pack was the chief cook in the mess hall at the Bingham Military School, which Mr. Bingham's grandfather operated in North Carolina. Tom Pack knew how to satisfy the appetites of a couple of hundred boys who spent hours every day on the drill ground. His Hobo Scramble was a hearty favorite. It was served for either breakfast or Sunday supper, with buttered grits and plenty of hot biscuits.

What You Will Need

4 eggs
2 tbsps. milk
2 tbsps. bacon drippings
2 ripe tomatoes

2 tbsps. chopped onions
½ tsp. salt
¼ tsp. pepper

1. Beat the eggs until light. Add the milk.
2. Melt the bacon drippings in a heavy iron skillet, add the onions, and cook them until they are golden.
3. Add the tomatoes in chunks and allow them to cook down until thick.
4. Pour the egg mixture into the tomatoes. Stir with a wooden spoon to keep soft, and add the salt and pepper to taste.
5. Serve with crisp bacon, crisp bits of salt pork, or thin slices of ham that have been warmed (but not fried) in butter.

VEGETABLE SOUP

A rich, homemade vegetable soup can be a meal in itself, and this recipe, from Ely Callaway of Burlington Industries, is both flavorful and filling — it calls for a whole chicken.

What You Will Need

Basic Stock: about 6½ quarts

A 12 quart kettle
A 3½ lb. chicken
2 lbs. raw or cooked beef or veal, bones and meat
2 tbsps. salt
3 tbsps. unsalted butter
1 tbsp. vegetable oil
5 medium-sized scraped carrots, cut in half lengthwise

6 medium-sized peeled onions, thickly sliced
5 stalks of celery with leaves
6 peppercorns
4 whole cloves
3 unpeeled cloves of garlic
8 sprigs parsley
2 bay leaves
½ tsp. thyme
4 leeks, thoroughly washed

1. Brown the chicken and meat in the butter and oil. When golden brown remove to a side dish while browning the carrots and onions.

2. Place the bones and meat back in the kettle and add the remaining vegetables, herbs, and seasonings.

3. Add cold water to cover by a full inch. Set over moderately high heat.

4. As the liquid approaches the simmer, scum will start to rise. You may remove it as it accumulates, or you may leave it, as Mr. Callaway and I prefer to do. Even though it makes the stock cloudy, there are many nutrients in that scum.

5. When the liquid is simmering, partially cover the kettle, and reduce the heat so that the liquid will be maintained at a very quiet simmer for 4 to 8 hours, or until you feel that the most has been simmered out of the ingredients. Correct seasoning.

6. Strain the stock into a large bowl, and refrigerate until the fat has hardened on the surface and can be removed easily. It is now ready to use. Whatever you do not wish to use right away may be frozen and defrosted as needed.

Add to 3 quarts of the basic stock (above) the following:

½ cup raw unwashed rice or ¾ cup
thin, tiny egg noodles (uncooked)
1½ cups canned tomatoes
   (if using fresh tomatoes
   remove skin and seeds)
1 package frozen okra,
   thawed and sliced
1 cup celery, diced
2 tsps. Worcestershire sauce
2 dashes Tabasco
salt and pepper to taste
juice of 1 lemon
Optional: ¾ cup very thinly sliced
   onion

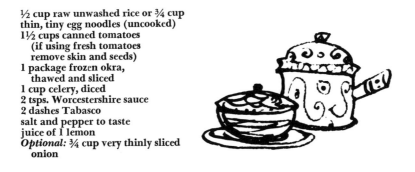

Bring the stock to a boil and add the celery, rice, and if used, onions. Reduce heat and maintain at a simmer for 15 minutes before adding all the remaining ingredients except the lemon juice, which should be added just before serving.

Simmer for an additional 15 minutes.

Remove from heat and add lemon juice.

Garnish with freshly cut parsley.

JOHNNY CAKES & DRIED BEEF GRAVY

The pleasures of international dining are at the beck and call of few of us — tycoon or mere gourmet — to the extent that they are of C. C. Tillinghast, President of Trans-World Airlines. At the drop of a hat this lucky man can appear in Tokyo for lunch, Hong Kong for dinner, Paris for breakfast.

But on a cold Sunday night, when the snow is falling on the sidewalks and windows frost up, and the mind begins to prepare itself to face the problems of a new week, here is what Mr. Tillinghast finds comfort in.

What You Will Need

1 cup Rhode Island Water Ground Corn Meal	1 8-ounce jar chipped beef
1¼ cups boiling water	3 tbsps. butter
1 tsp. salt	3 tbsps. flour
1 tsp. sugar	2 cups boiling milk

1. For the gravy, melt the butter in a heavy saucepan until it foams. Stir the flour and cook, stirring rapidly, for 2 minutes. Do not permit the mixture to brown.

2. Add the boiling milk, all at once, and stir over a low flame until you get a lovely sauce. This is the simplest process in the world, and the foundation of all good sauces.

3. Stir in the chipped beef and set the gravy aside (keep it covered to keep it warm).

4. Combine the cornmeal, salt, sugar, and add the boiling water. Mix well to form a thick batter.

5. On a medium hot, well-greased frying pan, drop the batter by tablespoonfuls.

6. Fry the johnny cakes for six minutes, turn, and fry for another five minutes.

7. Pour the gravy over the johnny cakes and serve.

SCALLOPINI — QUICK & EASY

The only American magazine that publishes a really comprehensive, easy-to-use guide to dining out in Europe is HOLIDAY — and so, with all this expertise, with this devotion to the great restaurants of Europe — and, incidentally, the great restaurants of the United States — HOLIDAY's publisher, Mr. John S. Connors, has a special interest in fine food.

168

But like all men who are confronted daily with the assorted pearls the world offers to the occasionally lucky, Mr. Connors, on a quiet Sunday night, likes this little dish — elegant, simple, light-hearted, and flavored with the magic of Rome. Rome!

What You Will Need

12 "scallops' of veal	¼ cup flour
1 tsp. salt	¼ tsp. minced garlic
½ tsp. pepper	½ cup butter

1. Salt and pepper the pieces of veal — and choose the whitest veal you can find.

2. Coat each piece of veal with a light covering of flour.

3. Heat the butter in an electric fry pan, together with the garlic, and then brown the veal — 2 minutes on each side.

4. Set the pan aside while you make the sauce.

For the Sauce:

1 package onion soup mix	1 large can mushrooms, with juice
1 package mushroom soup mix	1 cup dry white wine

1. Bring these ingredients to a boil, pour over the veal, and simmer for five minutes. Serve with rice, noodles, or mashed potatoes.

EASY STROGANOFF

Rose Morgan is one of the few women who have managed to found an empire. Helena Rubenstein did it. So did Elizabeth Arden. Rose Morgan, and the Rose Morgan House of Beauty, reflect the new wave, as everyone knows.

Miss Morgan's favorite recipe is beef stroganoff with wine sauce. What a classic this is — and how many ways there are to cook it. Here is a simple way that can't miss — and will amaze your guests.

1½ lbs. top round steak, ground twice	salt and pepper to taste
2 cups heavy cream	1 tbsp. vinegar
1 cup dry white wine	1 tbsp. paprika
¼ cup tomato sauce	¼ cup onions, minced
2 cups button mushrooms (canned)	1 cup beef broth
	¼ cup chopped parsley

1. Melt the butter in a deep, heavy frying pan until it foams.

2. Add the onions and ground beef and brown lightly.

3. Add the paprika, tomato sauce and mushrooms with their juice. Simmer for 2 minutes.

4. Sour the cream by mixing it with the vinegar. Add in driblets to the meat mixture.

5. Add the wine until you have a sauce of a moderately thick consistency.

6. Salt and pepper to taste, add the parsley; and simmer for 5 minutes before serving.

SWISS FONDUE

Another man of letters — Arnold Gingrich, the publisher of ESQUIRE — likes a simple Sunday supper best. His special touch is to limit the dinner to two persons (a typically seductive ESQUIRE ploy). Mr. Gingrich acquired this recipe during his residence on the shores of Lake Geneva, in the '40's. He considers the whole process a game, and I present it in his own words:

"These quantities make a meal for 2, a snack for 4.

"Once begun, stirring can't stop, so have everything ready before you approach the fire. Set up your chafing dish stand, and light the flame (this is for serving, not for cooking).

"Cut the FRENCH BREAD into 1 inch cubes and set out for dipping into the fondue.

"Mix into a paste 2 tablespoons FLOUR and 3 tablespoons COGNAC;

"Cut 1 pound of SWISS CHEESE into cubes ¼ inch square;

"Measure out 1½ cups WHITE WINE.

"Ready. Put cheese and wine into pan that can stand hot flame. Stir constantly over high flame on stove (flame of chafing dish isn't hot enough) until completely melted and of a soupy consistency, with no trace of cube forms on the cheese.

"Without faltering in your brisk stirring, add the flour-cognac mixture, and as soon as that is incorporated, remove fondue from the stove and put it over the chafing dish stand. (A plate warmer with one anemic candle is not hot enough to keep the fondue from becoming ropy and taffylike, and ultimately approaching the consistency of bubble gum.)

"Keep stirring. Now, each participant in turn spears his cube of French bread on the fork and stirs it across the center of the pan. When one guest removes his fork, the other must immediately get his in, stirring constantly until the next person is ready to take over.

"Two to four can play this game. If there are more than 4 people, there must be more than one fondue. The Swiss rule is that whoever allows his cube of bread to fall off his fork, into the fondue, must buy the next round of drinks.

"The French version is that whoever drops his bread must pay with a kiss. So the dish is as much of a sport as a meal."

170

Bright Ideas for Business Breakfasts
The Ideas:
Cheese Delight
Egg Stretcher De Luxe
French Toast with Sausages
Quiche Lorraine
Oyster Omelet
Shad Roe Mold
Croissants

The contributors: Newton N. Minow, Liebman, Williams, Bennett, Baird & Minow; J. P. McFarland, General Mills; Reed O. Hunt, Crown Zellerbach; Andrew Goodman, Bergdorf Goodman; Ben W. Heineman, Chicago & Northwestern Railroad.

CHEESE DELIGHT

It would be difficult to exaggerate the importance of having a good breakfast. That breakfast is the most important meal of the day is a platitude so often mouthed by nutrition experts that it has become a cliche. Yet the number of people who actually eat the minimum amount of food at breakfast suggested by the Department of Agriculture is shockingly small.

One of the reasons for this carelessness may be that breakfast is so frequently boring — the same dull food day after day, year after year. If one were required to eat a lobster every night, to the exclusion of all other food, in a few months he would have little interest in supper.

Eggs are the standard breakfast offering — they are high in protein, low in fat, easy to digest, and quick and easy to prepare. But show some imagination in cooking them. With business breakfasts growing more and more popular, the tycoon who gives them must learn to make them interesting. Cheese Delight is high in protein, easy to do, and comes out looking like a cheese souffle, though it is infinitely less complicated. Serve it with warm croissants, orange marmalade, steaming black coffee, and fresh fruit. This recipe comes from Newton N. Minow of Leibman, Williams, Bennett, Baird & Minow.

What You Will Need

5 slices of bread, buttered and cubed	2 cups milk
¾ lb. sharp cheddar cheese	½ tsp. salt
4 eggs	½ tsp. dry mustard
	½ tsp. pepper

1. Grate the cheese and beat the eggs slightly.

2. In a buttered, 1½ quart souffle dish, alternate a layer of bread with cheese.

3. Mix the eggs and mustard together with the milk and pour over the bread and cheese.

4. Add the salt and pepper. Let the mixture stand for 1 hour at room temperature. Bake it for one hour at 350°F and serve immediately.

OVERTON'S EGG STRETCHER DE LUXE

This recipe comes from Mr. W. W. Overton, Chairman of the Board of the Texas Bank & Trust Co. of Dallas, Texas. For it you will need:

6 tsps. chopped Jalapeno peppers	12 tbsps. cottage cheese
salt and pepper to taste	6 eggs

1. Heat the cottage cheese in the top of a double boiler.

2. Add the whole eggs, stirring gently but constantly, and cooking slowly and lightly.

3. Stir in the chopped Jalapeno peppers. Serve in prewarmed, individual covered casseroles.

CROISSANTS

Here is an American version of a famous French breakfast roll, the croissant. It is perfect for any breakfast, and may even be used with lunch or dinner. Serve the rolls hot and crisp with sweet butter and marmalade. This recipe comes from J. P. McFarland, President of General Mills Inc.

What You Will Need

2 pkgs. active dry yeast	**2 eggs**
¾ cup warm water (105 to 115 F)	**½ cup butter**
½ cup sugar	**4 cups Gold Medal Flour***
1 tsp. salt	**soft butter**

*Regular or wondra flour; if using self-rising flour, omit the salt.

1. Dissolve the yeast in warm water in a large mixing bowl.

2. Stir sugar, salt, eggs, ½ cup butter and half the flour into the yeast.

3. Add the remaining flour; mix until smooth.

4. Scrape the dough from the side of the bowl; cover the bowl with cloth and let the dough rise in a warm place (85°F) until it has doubled. This takes about an hour and a half.

5. Divide the dough in half; roll each part into a 12 inch circle a fourth of an inch thick.

6. Spread the surface with soft butter and slice each circle into 16 wedges.

7. Roll up each wedge, beginning at the rounded edge. Place the point side down on a greased baking sheet.

8. Curve the rolls to form crescents. Cover them with a cloth and let them rise until double in size — about 1 hour.

9. Heat the oven to 400°F. Bake 12 to 15 minutes or until the rolls are a rich, golden brown. Brush with butter and serve.

NOTE: This recipe makes 32 croissants. Leftover rolls may be wrapped and frozen for later use.

FRENCH TOAST

French toast is a particular favorite of tycoons, and many of them cook it themselves. This recipe is from Reed O. Hunt, Chairman of the Board of Crown Zellerbach Corporation.

What You Will Need

6 eggs
12 tbsps. milk
1 loaf whole wheat bread
½ cup butter

1. Beat the eggs and milk until well mixed.

2. Soak slices of bread in this mixture until you can barely pick it up in a spatula without breaking it.

3. Fry in butter until the juice stops coming out. Salt and pepper and serve in stacks with fried sausages.

WOODY'S OYSTER OMELET

This is a great omelet when oysters are in season. It was invented by Woodrow Wirsig, President of the Better Business Bureau of New York City. The recipe serves 2.

What You Will Need

1 cup fresh oysters	1 tbsp. milk
4 eggs	¼ cup butter
¼ cup onions, chopped	1 tbsp. salad oil
¼ cup pimientos	salt and pepper to taste

1. Chop the onions and pimientos finely and sauté them in a heavy iron skillet until the onions are golden.

2. Mix the onions and pimientos in a double boiler with the oysters, and heat the oysters until the skirts curl — about 5 minutes.

3. Beat the eggs and milk together with a wire whip. When the eggs are foamy and yellow, pour them into a frying pan containing ¼ cup foaming, melted butter.

4. Reduce heat under the frying pan. Shake the pan constantly while the eggs cook. When they appear to be browned underneath, but are still runny and creamy on top, add the chopped onion and oyster mixture, fold the omelet over, cut it in half, and serve.

SHAD ROE MOLD

At an important breakfast, during the course of a corporate merger, say, or when announcing a stock split, try this elegant favorite of Andrew Goodman, President of Bergdorf Goodman. Shad Roe appears to be a particular favorite of many tycoons — this is the third recipe for it in this book, and a variation of Mr. Goodman's earlier recipe for Shad Roe Monogram (see index).

What You Will Need

2 tbsps. butter	juice from ½ lemon
2 tbsps. flour	salt and pepper to taste
1 cup light cream	4 egg yolks
1 pair roe, canned or fresh	4 egg whites

1. Melt 2 tablespoons of butter in a heavy saucepan over a low flame.

2. When the butter foams, add 2 tbsps. of flour and stir until thick.

3. Add 1 cup boiling light cream and stir again until the mixture is thick. If you are using fresh roe, skin the pair and add to the sauce; if you are using canned roe, there is no skin.

4. Remove the roe and sauce mixture from the stove and cool. Add salt, pepper, and lemon juice to taste.

5. When the roe mixture is cool, add 4 yolks, one at a time, and stir thoroughly.

6. Beat the 4 egg whites stiff but not dry, and fold them in.

7. Pour the mixture into a buttered, covered ring mold. If your mold has no cover you may use aluminum foil.

8. Cook over a low flame on top of the stove for 30 minutes in a covered pan with a little water on the bottom to create steam.

9. Unmold and serve with poached eggs, bacon, and hollandaise or tomato sauce.

QUICHE LORRAINE

This classic recipe comes from Mr. Ben Heineman, Chairman of the Board of the Chicago & Northwest Railroad. Cooking is a bit out of Mr. Heineman's line, but eating is a greatly enjoyed past time.

What You Will Need

¾ pound bacon, crisply fried and crumbled
1 medium onion, diced
2 tbsps. bacon drippings
½ pound Swiss cheese, grated
1 single pie crust, unbaked

1 tbsp. flour
4 eggs
1 cup light cream
½ tsp. salt
¼ tsp. pepper
¼ tsp. nutmeg

1. Sauté the onion in bacon drippings until it is transparent. Drain it on a paper towel.

2. Sprinkle the flour over the grated Swiss cheese and toss well.

3. Beat the eggs lightly, add cream or milk, salt, pepper, and nutmeg. Mix well.

4. Add a layer of most of the onion and crumbled bacon to the unbaked pie shell, then a layer of the grated cheese, alternating these ingredients until none are left.

5. Pour the milk-egg mixture over the contents of the pie shell, sprinkling the reserved bacon on top.

6. Bake 35 to 45 minutes in a 375°F oven, or until a knife inserted near the center comes out clean.

About
California
Wines

The first California wines were made by padres at the Mission San Diego in 1769. The padres moved northward establishing missions and planting vineyards as far north as Sonoma. They discovered the California soil and climate ideal for growing grapes. In 1824 the first California wines were produced commercially. From then until 1918 California produced a wide variety of fine wines, which were shipped all over the world.

During the Prohibition years many of the vineyards were destroyed and the wineries fell into decay. After repeal, there was a great demand for wine, but because the industry lacked both capital and know-how, the goal in general was for volume rather than quality. It took years to build up the vineyards and rebuild the wineries.

However, in the last 30 years many of the California wine makers have replanted the vineyards with fine varieties, rebuilt and modernized their wineries and improved their wine-making processes. In the past 15 or 20 years California wineries have come to the fore to produce wine equal in many instances to the finest European wines. Not only I, but most knowledgeable people who are acquainted with wine, believe that, with the exception of a few chateau bottlings, the wines of California today are equal to, if not better, than most European wines and that they are distinctive wines in their own right.

Our wine industry is by no means at its maximum as far as quality is concerned. All the wine makers, including those who produce *vin ordinaire,* are trying, with new equipment, improved methods and greater controls, to produce wines that are finer in every respect. California wines are among the finest in the world. Enjoy them.

Trader Vic

THE
CALIFORNIA
WINELAND DISTRICTS

1. Sonoma - Mendocino 2. Napa Valley
3. Lodi District 4. Alameda - Contra Costa
5. Modesto - Ripon - Escalon
6. Santa Clara - Santa Cruz - San Benito
7. Fresno - San Joaquin 8. Cucamonga District

Winelands
of
California

Although only a single state, California ranks as a wine nation or, more accurately, as a group of wine nations. All the great grape varieties of France and Germany and many from Italy, Spain and Portugal are grown successfully within this large state.

From these aristocratic grapes come the counterparts of the great wines of Europe, yet they have an individual charm and character derived from the soil from which they spring. As Robert Louis Stevenson wrote, "The smack of California earth shall linger on the palate of your grandson."

The wide range of wine grape varieties that flourish in California is made possible by the differences in soil, climate, irrigation and cultivation methods that exist in the various wine areas. Somewhere in California every variety of wine grape can be planted with confidence.

California's finest table wines come from the valleys and foothills of the Central Coast Counties. The carefully selected bottles presented in this list come chiefly from the famous wineries within these areas.

Sonoma & Mendocino Counties

This is a large district, the vineyards of Mendocino being the most northerly in California. The lower and most distinguished section of this region, Sonoma, lies between Napa on the east and the Pacific Ocean.

Growing conditions in the easterly part of Sonoma are quite similar to those of Napa, but average temperatures are lower and on the ocean side there is apt to be more rain and fog.

There are more bonded wineries in Sonoma-Mendocino than in any of the other wine districts. They are found close to the cities and towns of Cloverdale, Asti, Healdsburg, Guerneville, Santa Rosa and Sonoma.

The table wines of this area are rightfully considered to be among the best in California.

Sonoma & Mendocino Counties
1 Italian Swiss Colony
2 Korbel Champagne Cellars
3 Martini & Prati Wines
4 Samuele Sebastiani
5 Buena Vista Vineyards

Napa
County

Napa Valley is considered by many to be the outstanding of the four great table wine districts which comprise the North Coast area of California.

The valley is about 35 miles long, its greatest width about five miles. On the south it borders on San Pablo Bay, on the north it is pinched off by mountains at Calistoga. Both east and west borders are formed by mountain ridges with the highest peaks approximately 2,600 feet.

Surprisingly the warmest part of the Napa Valley is the northern part near Calistoga and the coolest is the area south of the city of Napa. Thus, even within this small area there are differences in the wines produced from grapes grown in various parts of the valley.

Napa County

1 Schramsberg Vineyards 5 The Christian Brothers
2 Hanns Kornell Cellars 6 Beringer Brothers
3 Souverain Cellars 7 Louis Martini
4 Charles Krug Winery 8 Beaulieu Vineyards
9 Inglenook Vineyards

Alameda & Contra Costa
Counties

The upper section of Contra Costa County is best known for its red wines, while Alameda excels in white wines.

The Livermore Valley of Alameda is a famous wine region, the soil and climate being especially favorable for the growing of distinguished white wine grapes. Some of the outstanding vineyards have a gravelly consistency that appears to impart a special and intriguing character to such varieties as Chardonnay, Grey Riesling, Sauvignon Blanc and Semillon.

While the white varieties predominate, some red wines of distinction are also made in this district. The principal wine centers are Martinez (Contra Costa), Livermore and Mission San Jose.

Alameda & Contra Costa
Counties

1 J. E. Digardi Winery
2 Wente Brothers
3 Concannon Vineyards
4 Weibel Champagne Vineyards

Santa Clara, Santa Cruz & San Benito Counties

These adjoining counties, Santa Clara and Santa Cruz, are generally considered as one wine district with Santa Cruz Mountains forming an intervening border. Together with San Benito, which lies below them, they form the largest and most southerly district in the Central Coast area.

Many of the vineyards in this district are planted on the slopes of the foothills, although there are important vineyards in the valleys.

Here, as in Napa Valley, the soil and climate are ideal for growing many fine wine grape varieties.

Felton and Soquel in Santa Cruz county, Santa Clara, San Jose, Saratoga and Los Gatos in Santa Clara county, Hollister and Paicines in San Benito county are the principal centers of this outstanding wine district. Recently Monterey county has become an important new area for grape growing.

Santa Clara, Santa Cruz & San Benito Counties
1 Martin Ray Inc.
2 Paul Masson Champagne Cellars
3 Novitiate of Los Gatos
4 San Martin Vineyards
5 S. Martinelli
6 Almaden Vineyards

Vintage
Years

Mother nature is a law unto herself and prone to moods beyond the ken of man. As there are pronounced changes in climate and weather throughout the world from year to year, the growing conditions in wine nations will vary. In Europe's wine-producing countries where only one wine grape variety or a group of varieties are grown in a limited area and where there is a wide range in climatic conditions from one year to another, a reliable vintage chart is often a great aid to potential buyers of European wines.

In California, unlike the wine countries of Europe, many varieties of wine grapes are grown in more than one wine producing area, thus enabling wineries in different areas to produce the same type of wine. As each area has its own climate and growing conditions, one area may produce a wine that is superior one year to that of another area. For example, the Pinot Noir of Napa county may be better in one year than the same type of wine produced in Sonoma county, or Alameda county. For this reason and because there is less difference in climatic conditions from one year to the next, any attempt to provide a general vintage chart for all California wines would not only be difficult but confusing.

There is no question about it. I am not a connoisseur of wine and my ability to judge it is limited. But somebody has to make a selection and I have asked a few of my friends, from time to time, to pass along their opinions.

We have been diligent and sincere. We may have made some mistakes, but certainly not intentionally. There are, without doubt, other wines of equal quality which have not been brought to our attention.

This is my California Wine Selection. The stars which denote the ratings represent my advisors' opinions and mine. They are not intended to be arbitrary; others may differ.

For the guidance of our patrons we have classified our special selections as follows:

   ☆   Wine with a particularly distinctive character.

 ☆ ☆   Exceptional wines with fully developed flavors.

☆ ☆ ☆   The finest.

Trader Vic

CHAMPAGNES
AND
SPARKLING WINES

Champagne

Champagnes are the most versatile of wines. They can be served as an aperitif, with most foods, or at the end of the meal. The best are naturally fermented in the bottle. California Champagne is made from some of the finest varieties of grapes grown in the state. There are some made only from white grapes known as Blanc de Blancs.

200 ALMADEN, Brut, n. v.
201 ALMADEN, Blanc de Blancs, 1962 Cuvee ☆ ☆
202 BEAULIEU, Brut, 1962 ☆ ☆ ☆
203 HANNS KORNELL, Brut, n. v. ☆
204 KORBEL, Brut, n. v. ☆
205 KORBEL, Sec., n. v.
206 PAUL MASSON, Brut, n. v. ☆
207 BEAULIEU, Special Reserve ☆ ☆
208 SCHRAMSBERG, Blanc de Blancs, 1965 ☆ ☆

Sparkling Wine

These beautiful pink and red wines, as produced in California, go well with many dishes. The best have a fruity and lively character and are popular with many Americans.

215 BEAULIEU, Champagne Rose, 1958 ☆ ☆

216 KORBEL, Rouge, n. v. ☆

217 PAUL MASSON, Sparkling Burgundy, n. v.

WHITE
DINNER
WINES

Chardonnay

Also called Pinot Chardonnay, this is the outstanding white wine grape grown in the Champagne, Chablis, Cote D'Or and Maconnais districts of France. Certain favored vineyards in the North Coast area of California produce superlative, full-bodied and rich wines with a characteristic aroma.

220 CHARLES KRUG, N. V. ☆ ☆
221 LOUIS MARTINI, 1961 ☆
222 PAUL MASSON, N. V.
223 WENTE BROS., Estate Bottled, 1964 ☆ ☆
224 STONY HILL, 1965 ☆ ☆
225 ALMADEN, Estate Bottled, 1964
     HANZELL, 1965

White Riesling

Often called Johannisberg, the California name for the variety which is responsible for the great wines of the Rhine and Moselle in Germany. These wines have a fruity and flowery character, which is much appreciated.

230 ALMADEN, Estate Bottled, 1960

231 CHARLES KRUG, N. V. ☆ ☆

232 CHRISTIAN BROS., n. v.

233 LOUIS MARTINI, 1964 ☆

234 SOUVERAIN, n. v. ☆ ☆

WHITE DINNER WINES

Sylvaner

Often called Franken Riesling in California. This variety is widely grown in Germany and Alsace. In California its highly-prized wines are soft with a slightly aromatic character.

    240 **ALMADÉN**, n. v. ☆

    241 **BEAULIEU**, Estate Bottled, 1962 ☆ ☆

    242 **CHARLES KRUG**, n. v. ☆

Grey Riesling

This is an early-ripening variety whose exact origin is not known. In California it produces soft, early maturing wines with a distinctive and spicy aroma. Long a favorite in the Bay Region.

    250 **ALMADÉN**, n. v.

    251 **BUENA VISTA**, 1961

    252 **CHARLES KRUG**, n. v. ☆

    253 **WENTE BROS.**, n. v. ☆

Gewurztraminer

A well-known variety in Alsace and Southern Germany. In California its wines are characterized by their spicy, almost Muscat-like character. Particularly appropriate with seasoned food.

    260 **ALMADÉN**, n. v. ☆

    261 **CHARLES KRUG**, n. v. ☆

    262 **LOUIS MARTINI**, 1962 ☆ ☆

WHITE DINNER WINES

Semillon

This variety (with Sauvignon Blanc) makes the great Bordeaux white wines. As a California varietal wine, it has charm and distinction; a sturdy flavor and mild aroma.

270 CHARLES KRUG, n. v.

271 CHRISTIAN BROS., n. v. ☆

272 CRESTA BLANCA (Premier) sweet, n. v. ☆ ☆ ☆

273 WENTE BROS., n. v. ☆

Sauvignon Blanc

This variety is used extensively (usually with Semillon) in Bordeaux. In favored vineyards in California, it produces wines of very high quality, dry but rich and fullbodied. It has one of the most characteristic varietal aromas of any of the California white wines.

280 ALMADÉN, n. v. ☆

281 CHRISTIAN BROS., n. v. ☆ ☆

282 WENTE BROS., 1963 ☆ ☆ ☆

WHITE DINNER WINES

Chenin Blanc

Also called White Pinot. The California wines from this variety have a moderately distinctive aroma but a fresh and grapy taste. Some are dry and others slightly sweet.

290 ALMADÉN, n. v.

291 CHARLES KRUG, n. v. ☆ ☆

292 INGLENOOK, 1964 ☆

Other Distinctive White Wines

300 CHABLIS, Beaulieu, 1964

301 CHABLIS, Charles Krug, n. v. ☆

302 EMERALD DRY, Paul Masson, n. v. ☆

303 GREEN HUNGARIAN, Souverain, n. v.

304 PINOT BLANC, Wente Bros., 1964 ☆

305 WHITE PINOT, Souverain, n. v. ☆ ☆

ROSÉ
WINES

Rosé

These beautiful, light pink wines may be served with almost any dish. In California they are produced mainly from Grenache or Gamay grapes, but other varieties are also used. Their chief charm is their grapy and refreshing flavor.

310 ALMADÉN, Estate Bottled, 1964 ☆

311 BEAULIEU, 1966

312 CHARLES KRUG, n. v. ☆

313 LOUIS MARTINI, n. v.

314 WENTE BROS., n. v. ☆ ☆

RED DINNER WINES

❦

Cabernet Sauvignon

Most connoisseurs believe that the finest red California wines are produced from this variety. They are characterized by their distinctive varietal aroma and their increasing bouquet and quality over long periods of aging.

320 ALMADEN, Estate Bottled, 1960
321 BEAULIEU, Estate Bottled, 1961 ☆
322 BEAULIEU
    (Georges de Latour, Private Reserve) 1962 ☆
323 BEAULIEU
    (Georges de Latour, Private Reserve) 1961 ☆
324 BEAULIEU
    (Georges de Latour, Private Reserve) 1960 ☆ ☆
325 BEAULIEU
    (Georges de Latour, Private Reserve) 1959 ☆ ☆
326 BUENA VISTA, Cask 109, Estate Bottled, n. v.
327 CHARLES KRUG, Vintage Selection, 1960 ☆
328 CHARLES KRUG, Vintage Selection, 1959 ☆ ☆
329 CHARLES KRUG, Vintage Selection, 1958 ☆ ☆
330 CHARLES KRUG, Vintage Selection, 1957 ☆ ☆ ☆
331 CRESTA BLANCA, n. v.
332 INGLENOOK, Estate Bottled, 1962
333 LOUIS MARTINI, 1963 ☆
334 LOUIS MARTINI, Private Reserve, 1957 ☆ ☆
335 LOUIS MARTINI, Private Reserve, 1955 ☆ ☆ ☆

RED DINNER WINES

Pinot Noir

This is the principal red wine grape variety of the Burgundy region of France. In favored vineyards of California, its wines are noted for their suave and distinctive character which improves with moderate aging.

340 ALMADEN, Estate Bottled, 1960
341 BEAULIEU, Estate Bottled, 1962 ☆
342 CHARLES KRUG, 1962
343 CHARLES KRUG, 1961 ☆ ☆
344 CHARLES KRUG, 1959 ☆ ☆ ☆
345 LOUIS MARTINI, Private Reserve, n. v. ☆
346 LOUIS MARTINI, Special Selection, 1962 ☆ ☆
347 WEIBEL, n. v.
348 WENTE BROS , n. v. ☆

Gamay and Gamay Beaujolais

These varieties, grown chiefly in the North and Central Coast areas, produce fruity wines with a distinctive grapy aroma. Generally they mature early and should be drunk young.

360 GAMAY, Inglenook, 1964

361 GAMAY, Charles Krug, 1963 ☆

362 GAMAY BEAUJOLAIS, Paul Masson, n. v. ☆

RED DINNER WINES

Zinfandel

This variety is truly Californian since its European counterpart has not been identified. Though grown throughout the state, the finer wines come from the hillside vineyards in the North Coast area. They have a very distinctive varietal aroma which is often characterized as berry-like.

370 **BUENA VISTA**, n. v. ☆

371 **CHARLES KRUG**, 1959 ☆ ☆

372 **CRESTA BLANCA**, n. v.

373 **LOUIS MARTINI**, 1963 ☆ ☆

374 **LOUIS MARTINI**, Private Reserve, 1956 ☆ ☆ ☆

375 **LOUIS MARTINI**, Private Reserve, 1955 ☆ ☆ ☆

Other Distinctive Red Wines

380 BURGUNDY, Beaulieu, Estate Bottled, 1964

381 BURGUNDY Wente Bros., n. v.

382 MOUNTAIN BARBERA, Louis Martini, 1962 ☆ ☆

383 MOUNTAIN BARBERA
　　　Louis Martini, Private Reserve, 1958 ☆ ☆ ☆

APERITIF
AND
DESSERT
WINES

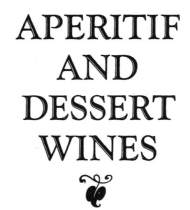

Aperitif and Dessert Wine

Spain and Portugal are the respective sources of classic Sherry and Port. These and other aperitif and dessert types are also well made in California. We recommend our selections.

390 **TRIPLE CREAM SHERRY, Cresta Blanca** ☆ ☆

391 **CREAM SHERRY, Inglenook**

392 **COCKTAIL SHERRY, Almadén** ☆

393 **COCKTAIL SHERRY, Christian Bros.**

394 **DRY SHERRY, Louis Martini** ☆

395 **RARE DRY SHERRY, Paul Masson**

396 **TAWNY PORT, Louis Martini**

397 **TINTA RUBY PORT, Almadén**

400 MOSCATO AMABILE, Louis Martini ☆ ☆
No explanation can be given for this outstanding Muscat dessert wine.

INDEX OF RECIPES

196

DESSERTS

MISCELLANEOUS

Bon Appétit!